Why Did This Happen to Me?

Ray Pritchard

HARVEST HOUSE PUBLISHERS

EUGENE, OREGON

Cover design by Koechel Peterson & Associates, Inc., Minneapolis, Minnesota

WHY DID THIS HAPPEN TO ME?
Formerly titled *The God You Can Trust*
Copyright © 2003 by Ray Pritchard
Published by Harvest House Publishers
Eugene, Oregon 97402

Library of Congress Cataloging-in-Publication Data

Pritchard, Ray, 1952–
    [God you can trust]
    Why did this happen to me? / Ray Pritchard.
        p. cm.
    Originally published: The God you can trust. Eugene, Or. : Harvest House Publishers, c2003.
    ISBN-13: 978-0-7369-1699-8 (pbk.)
    ISBN-10: 0-7369-1699-7
    1. Trust in God. I. Title.
    BV4637.P757 2006
    248.8'6—dc22   2005019198

Printed in the United States of America

05 06 07 08 09 10 11 12 / DPS-MS / 10 9 8 7 6 5 4 3 2 1

To Cliff and Phyllis Raad
with love and affection

Contents

Whom Can We Trust?

When it comes to the difficult circumstances of life—the things that devastate our heart and leave us groping for answers—whom or what can we trust? What can we cling to and lean upon when a loved one inexplicably dies...our marriage crumbles...our children rebel? What about good Christians who suddenly find everything going wrong in life—seriously wrong? Whom or what can we trust for help?

In the end, the answer is God and God alone. This book comes out of a quarter century as a pastor observing Christians struggling to hold on to their faith in the midst of confusing circumstances, unexplainable tragedy, and (very often) their own foolish mistakes. I am writing not as an ivory-tower theologian but as a pastor who spends his days pointing people back to God as their only hope.

The idea for this book was born in my heart several years ago when, for reasons that I don't quite recall just now, I felt a need to investigate the faithfulness of God. I was fascinated to discover that while there are many books about God, there are very few that focus exclusively on His faithfulness. But my own studies revealed that this is a major biblical theme. Those studies led to a series of sermons that eventually became the foundation for this book.

I received an e-mail from a woman I hardly know reflecting on what the faithfulness of God means to her.

Although she was raised in a godly home, she never envisioned the struggles that come with being a single woman in her early 30s. She always thought she would someday marry a man like her father and live happily ever after. In her own words, "I thought I deserved to be a happily married Christian housewife. Maybe this doesn't make any sense to you, but to me it was sort of a promise from God to women. I just couldn't find the verse." At this point she placed a little smiley-face symbol in her e-mail. She went on to mention the sadness she felt over various mistakes she had made out of the sheer agony of loneliness. "The mental games that Satan likes to play at times of despair have completely overwhelmed me to the point of exhaustion."

Then comes the good news. The truth that God finishes what He starts (which we will consider in chapter 9 of this book) changed her life:

> I often feel like I am just trudging through my days, waiting for something miraculous to happen, just hoping that I won't fall into some other great sin. "If I could just make it to Sunday, then I will be okay" has been my plea for many years. But now knowing that God actually wants to do something with me has rekindled a little more faith for my future. God's truly amazing grace is so simple when understood—it is all based on His love, and no matter what I do (or don't do), no matter who I struggle with becoming, and no matter what I do to mess everything up, He still has a plan for me. What an awesome God I serve.

It is right at this point that two lines of truth intersect. Our world is indeed unpredictable, uncertain, and sometimes very dangerous. We're reminded of that truth every time we turn on the television or pick up a newspaper. Today's worries aren't going away anytime soon, and if they do disappear, other threats will take their place. And in these early days of the twenty-first century, we all struggle with the personal questions of life and death, family, career and relationships, what we are doing versus what we should be doing, and the inevitable stresses of marriage, divorce, singleness, and bringing children into a world like this and raising them with faith, hope, and love. Add to that the problems of sickness, doubt, fear, and the fact that no one knows what tomorrow will bring. As a friend said to me yesterday, "God didn't give me a videotape." The future is a mystery to all of us.

And so we are left with God. Read that sentence again slowly. Let its truth sink into your soul. Everything else I'm going to say in this book is but an expansion of that one truth. *We begin with God and we end with God, and He is our only hope between the beginning and the end.* If you believe that already, I hope that your faith is strengthened even more as you read through this book to the last chapter. If you don't believe that, or if the events of life have shaken your faith in God, then my advice is to read this book slowly and thoughtfully. In every crisis of life we can choose to believe, or we can give in to doubt and despair. Whenever we are ready, we can move beyond our circumstances to discover that God was there all along. If that sounds good to you, then turn the page, and let's get started on the journey to know the God you can trust.

CHAPTER 1

The Lord Who Is Faithful

The call came while I was getting ready to go to work. I must have been in another room because I didn't hear the phone ring, so the caller left a message on our answering machine. When I listened to the message, I heard a man's voice say that their 12-day-old baby had died during the night. Would I come to the hospital and pray with them?

A few minutes later I pulled into the hospital parking lot and the thought came to me that there is no greater tragedy than the death of a child. I wondered as I waited for the elevator what I would say when I finally saw the parents. A nurse met me and took me to a small room. When I walked in, I saw the mother and father sitting together, holding the body of their infant son. He had died a few hours earlier.

The medical story was quite simple. He had been born almost five months early, weighing less than a pound and a half. The doctors had told the parents early on that despite their best efforts, and some amazingly advanced technology, there was only a slim chance for survival. Little Christopher hung on for 12 days, fighting through one crisis after another. Finally, his little body could fight no longer.

Although I stayed with the parents for over an hour, most of that time is a blur in my mind. I remember the father saying that his son had long skinny legs just like his. The mother wept as she held her baby and repeated, "Why did this happen?" Near the end of my visit, I held my hand under the baby's head and thought about all the dreams and all the prayers that had been invested in him. Now he was gone almost before he arrived. "God must have a reason," the mother said. "He has a reason, doesn't He?"

As I am writing these words, I just paused and looked up from my computer and thought to myself, *This is the hardest moment*. I have been a pastor for over 25 years, and in that time I have been privileged to walk with multitudes of people through some very dark moments of life. And I want you to know that I do not use the word *privileged* lightly. Like most pastors, no two of my days are exactly alike. Some days are spent studying the Bible, others seem to disappear in an unending series of meetings and phone calls and a blizzard of church trivia that is hard to remember, much less to explain. But there are moments when every pastor deals with what you might call Ultimate Reality—the real stuff of life and death, of joy and sorrow, of gain and loss, those moments when we all learn once again that time is but the nursery of eternity.

That day in that cramped hospital room, sitting next to grieving parents who held their dead baby in their hands, was one of those moments when I remember why I became a pastor in the first place. And yet it is also the hardest moment of all. When tragedy strikes, the question always comes sooner or later: Why did this happen? Why would God allow it? Why didn't God stop it? I will say simply and honestly that I do not always have what seems a sufficient answer to that question. Not that I do not have an answer, or that my answer is untrue. I simply mean that the answer I give is the one that Christians have given for 2000 years. It is good and true and biblical. It's just that in the moment that the question is uttered, the answer does not always seem sufficient. But, then, what answer *would* be sufficient when you hold your child, your firstborn, in your hands and realize that he did not live long enough to open his eyes?

I do not believe in easy answers to hard questions. Easy answers may get us off the hook in the short run, but precisely because they are "easy," they often hurt more in the long run. Over the years I have discovered that there are answers that will give us strength to go on, and there is abundant hope to be found in the Word of God. I hope to share some of those answers with you in the pages that follow. And, as you'll discover, I don't mind saying, "I don't know" when I really don't know. When I told those parents that I didn't know why their child died, I meant it quite literally. I know there are various medical explanations that provide some perspective regarding premature birth. But as to why God allowed that to happen to this particular baby, that is a mystery that, as far as I can tell, is completely hidden from us. We can speculate, and perhaps our speculations will provide some comfort, but as the years pass, I find a growing sense of comfort in admitting that there are some things (many things, really) that we simply cannot fully explain.

God and Change

The flip side of that truth is just as important. After a quarter century as a pastor, there are some things that I believe more fervently now than when I started in the ministry. Foremost among them is the faithfulness of God. *By that I mean that I believe in a God who cares for His people and who always keeps His word.* When I was a teenager in Alabama, I spent a week at a Methodist church camp. This was during the revolutionary days of the 1960s when the talk was of LSD, the Beatles, hippies, the Vietnam War, and protests in the streets. No one had heard of fax machines, virtual reality, or compact discs. Even though I was too young to understand it all, I remember feeling that this was the most exciting time in history to be alive. Of that long-forgotten week, I remember only the theme: "God and Change." It was a fitting slogan for the psychedelic age, the message being that only two things are constant: God (who never changes) and change (which is always with us). More than 30 years later, that statement seems entirely true. In a fickle, ever-changing world, only God never changes. He alone is entirely faithful, all the time. Consider the following verses from the Bible:

> He passed in front of Moses, proclaiming, "The LORD, the LORD, the compassionate and gracious God, slow to anger, abounding in love and faithfulness..." (Exodus 34:6).

> Know therefore that the LORD your God is God; he is the faithful God, keeping his covenant of love to a thousand generations of those who love him and keep his commands (Deuteronomy 7:9).

> This is what the LORD says—the Redeemer and Holy One of Israel—to him who was despised and abhorred by the nation, to the servant of rulers: "Kings will see you and rise up, princes will see and bow down, because of the LORD, who is faithful, the Holy One of Israel, who has chosen you" (Isaiah 49:7).

> The one who calls you is faithful and he will do it (1 Thessalonians 5:24).

> Let us hold unswervingly to the hope we profess, for he who promised is faithful (Hebrews 10:23).

Let's isolate the key phrases:

"Abounding in love and faithfulness"

"He is the faithful God"

"The LORD, who is faithful"

"The one who calls you is faithful"

"He who promised is faithful"

The Ever-Faithful God

Many other Bible verses can be added to this list to bring home the point that God is faithful.

But is it true? An old friend from another time and another place sent me a message. The last several years have been difficult for him because of problems with a wayward child. He wrote to say that the child will soon be sentenced to serve time in a juvenile detention facility. Then he wrote, "God has been ever faithful to us and her through this period of 'the spirit of Cain' (irrational and total rebellion). Perhaps she will yet become like the prodigal in repenting." Here is a man who has discovered—and is daily learning anew—the truth that God is faithful even in the midst of a heartbreaking family crisis.

Not long ago my friend Bruce Thorn called from his home in Sheffield, Alabama. During our conversation he mentioned that God had been speaking to his heart on a certain subject. He had asked several other friends about it, and they confirmed it to him. The message was this: *God is challenging His people to trust Him.* In a world where every day brings new revelations of chaos and moral confusion, we need to ask ourselves if we really trust God. It's one thing to say, "I trust in the Lord" when the sun is shining and all the bills are paid. It's something else to trust Him when the dark clouds settle round us and the bill collectors are at the door.

Whom or what can we trust? *We live in an era of planned obsolescence.* We buy a car knowing that it will last a handful of years. We buy new clothes knowing they won't last more than a year or two. It's worse with computers. Several years ago I purchased a whiz-bang, superfast computer from an Internet auction house. I bought it knowing that technological advances would quickly make it obsolete. Today I use it only with great reluctance because my "superfast" computer is now a dinosaur, a relic from the past, like the Edsels in a Memorial Day parade.

Add to that the uncertainty of life. Companies downsize. Bosses say, "Let's talk about your future because it's not here." Friends move away, marriages dissolve, children leave home, and our health doesn't last forever. Friends and loved ones pass away. And we live in fear of cancer or a sudden heart attack.

In this world of ceaseless change, God is the only constant. As Moses declared, "He is the faithful God." That's an important word for today. The Marine Corps motto is *Semper Fidelis* (or shortened to *Semper Fi*)—Always faithful. But how many people do you know who do exactly what they say? Before you answer, let me rephrase the question. How many people do you know who do exactly what they say every single time? Let me rephrase it again. How many people do you know who do exactly what they say every single time and do it with such thoroughness and perfection that you never have to worry about anything they say or do? Again, before you answer, let me ask it this way: *How many people do you know who, no matter what the circumstances and no matter how they feel, will always do exactly what they say every single time and do it with such thoroughness and perfection that you never have to worry about anything they say or do because you know if they say it, they will definitely do it without fail, without change, and without excuse?*

The answer to any question depends on how you ask it. Most of us probably think we know some people who do exactly what they say. That is, we all know some reliable people who seem very dependable to us. But in the end, the question is not about reliable or very dependable people. *It's really not about people at all because no person could meet all the qualifications of the last question, which is really about God.* He alone is 100 percent faithful 100 percent of the time.

A World of Broken Promises

We live in a world of broken promises. Leaders pledge peace and secretly make plans for a war. Marriages end over trivial disputes. And presidents wag their finger and say, "I didn't," knowing full well that they did. I happened to catch a few minutes of a national radio talk show where the host discussed several prominent celebrities whose personal hypocrisies have been exposed. He then asked a penetrating question: "Is there anyone out there who is what he claims to be?" If you're looking in this world, the answer is no. But if you look outside this world, you discover that God is what He claims to be.

- God is not a man, that he should lie, nor a son of man, that he should change his mind; does he speak and then not act? Does he promise and not fulfill? (Numbers 23:19).

- ...the only true God (John 17:3).

- God...is faithful (1 Corinthians 1:9).

- God is faithful (1 Corinthians 10:13).

- He is faithful (1 John 1:9).

- ...him who is true (1 John 5:20).

When taken together, these verses establish that God's faithfulness is not some minor or secondary part of God's character. *To say that God is faithful goes to the core of who God really is.* He keeps His word because if He didn't, He wouldn't be God! We could multiply similar verses in every direction because all that God does rests on His faithfulness and every blessing we receive comes because He is faithful to keep His promises to us. If God were not faithful, we could not be saved, would not dare to pray, would have no sure hope for the future, and would go down in death in desperate fear wondering if God will keep His promises. But we can live in faith and die in hope precisely because our God is faithful.

Because God is faithful, there are three certainties we can lean upon at all times.

Every Word He Says Is True

The Bible contains several words for *truth*. One of the most important is the Hebrew word *emet,* which means "stability, firmness, or certainty." We get the English word *amen* from the Hebrew *emet.* Every time we say, "Amen," we are really saying, "It is certain" or, "Yes, it is absolutely true." Therefore, to say "God is true" is the same as saying "God is faithful." Here's a simple definition: *God's faithfulness means that because He is the truth, everything He says and does is certain.* That means He is 100 percent reliable 100 percent of the time. In the words of Lewis Sperry Chafer: "He not only advances and confirms that which is true, but in faithfulness abides by his promises, and executes every threat or warning he has made." He says what He means and means what He says and therefore does everything He says He will do. He does not fail, forget, falter, or vacillate. If He says it, He means it, and you can stake your life upon it.

And where will we find the true words of God? In the Bible. God has given us an entire book filled with His words. If that be so, then our job is to read that book. Study it. Memorize it. Learn it. Build our life upon it. We are to love God's Word to the point that His words flow through us like the blood that flows through our veins. God says, "Amen" over every word He speaks. This means that we can trust the entire Bible because it all comes from God. Whether we read in Genesis or Joshua or 2 Kings or Ezra or Lamentations or Luke or Galatians or 2 Thessalonians or 3 John or Revelation, we can trust what we read because God is the ultimate author and every word He speaks is true.

Several years ago, as the twentieth century wound to a close and the twenty-first century was dawning, I wondered to myself what our congregation could do to properly celebrate the beginning of a new millennium. It would not do to call this a once-in-a-lifetime event. It would be more like once-in-40-lifetimes. None of us were around when the calendar changed from 999 to 1000, and none of us would be around a thousand years hence to mark the change from the year 2999 to 3000. So how exactly should we celebrate such an unusual event? After some deliberation, we decided to have a Bible reading marathon. For the last 90 hours of 1999, hundreds of people, from little children to senior citizens, joined in the public reading of the Bible from the pulpit in our sanctuary, from the first verse of Genesis 1 to the last verse of Revelation 22. We started at 6:00 A.M. on December 28, 1999, and continued around the clock until midnight, December 31. This was an unbroken reading of God's Word from beginning to end with no stopping at all. No music, no prayer times, no testimonies, no sermons, no stops for personal commentary, no stops for any reason. One person after another read the Word of God. When one person finished, another continued. We read through Genesis, Exodus, Leviticus, and we eventually read through 2 Kings,

Job, Isaiah, Daniel, and Zechariah. As I recall, it took us over two days of reading to reach the New Testament. On we went, in 15-minute segments, reading Matthew, Mark, Luke, John, Acts, and the epistles of Paul. The reading continued morning, noon, and night. Audience size varied from two or three to 30 or 40 or more. As we neared the end on New Year's Eve, hundreds of people came to listen to the reading of the book of Revelation. A large clock next to the pulpit counted down the hours, minutes, and seconds. When we finally reached midnight, we were at the last few verses of Revelation 22. When we finished, the choir sang "The Hallelujah Chorus" from Handel's *Messiah*. The Millennium 2000 Bible Reading Marathon was covered by radio and television and by Chicago newspapers and by the *Boston Globe*.

The reporters kept asking why we would do something like this. We told them we did it to proclaim our confidence that God's Word is true and that every part of it deserved to be read and believed as we entered a new millennium. We wanted the world to know that the same message that has carried the church for 2000 years will take us into the future. Looking back, that 90 hours we spent reading the Bible seems like one of the most significant things our church has ever done. It reminded us all over again that because God is faithful, His Word can be trusted. It's all true, every part of it, from first to last.

Here is a second certainty connected to God's faithfulness...

Every Promise Will Be Kept

Because God is faithful, He keeps every promise He makes. Have you taken the time to trace God's promises through the Bible? If you haven't, I recommend that you begin underlining every promise you find. When did God make the promise? To whom was it given? What were the conditions? How was it fulfilled? How does it apply to us today? There are thousands of promises covering every situation we face—including salvation, the forgiveness of sin, prayer, marriage, children, disappointment, insecurity, and a whole host of other issues. Second Corinthians 1:20 says that "no matter how many promises God has made, they are 'Yes' in Christ. And so through him the 'Amen' is spoken by us to the glory of God." Eugene Peterson (*The Message*) translates the first phrase this way: "Whatever God has promised gets stamped with the Yes of Jesus." When God the Father makes a promise, God the Son says from heaven, "Yes, it is so." God the Holy Spirit writes the promise in the Word and then applies that Word to our hearts. Thus, all three Persons of the Godhead unite in bringing God's promises to us. That's why when we read a promise of God, we can truly say, "Amen." If God has said it, we can count on it.

Many years ago I came across this powerful summary statement in Joshua 21:43-45:

> The LORD gave Israel all the land he had sworn to give their forefathers, and they took possession of it and settled there. The LORD gave them rest on every side, just as he had sworn to their forefathers. Not one of their enemies withstood them; the LORD handed all their enemies over to them. Not one of all the LORD's good promises to the house of Israel failed; every one was fulfilled.

What a grand statement that is! If we go back and read Joshua carefully, we see how God kept His promises:

—*Not quickly* (it took seven years)

—*Not without a struggle* (there were many battles)

—*Not without some failure along the way* (such as the sin of Achan in Joshua 7)

—Not without some loss of life (many soldiers died in various battles)

But what God said, He did. No one could have known in advance how it would happen. But it did. In the end, the Israelites were totally victorious.

Gladys Aylward served as a missionary in China before World War II. When the Japanese army invaded northern China, she was forced to flee Yangcheng, taking with her 100 orphans. As she led the orphans into the mountains, she despaired of ever making it to safety. After a sleepless night, she was reminded by a 13-year-old girl of the story of Moses and the parting of the Red Sea. "'But I am not Moses,' she replied. 'Of course you aren't,' the girl said, 'but Jehovah is still God.'" Is that not a word for today? No matter what mountains may loom before us, God is still God, and we can trust in Him.

Do you feel squeezed by your circumstances? Dwell much on the promises of God. Read the promises. Write them down. Put them where you can see them in the morning when you wake up. Put them on the dashboard of your car. Tell them to your friends. Most of all, repeat the promises of God to the Lord when you pray. Stand on God's promises—and do not let yourself be moved.

Every Trial Has a Purpose

Nothing happens by chance to the children of God. I have observed that when hard times come, we tend to think that God has forgotten about us or that what has happened is a mistake or has no purpose. And I have seen that God's people can endure almost anything if they know there is a reason for it.

Consider these four truths from Scripture:

1. *He knows what I am going through*—"He knows the way that I take; when he has tested me, I will come forth as gold" (Job 23:10).

2. *He uses my trials to help me grow*—"We also rejoice in our sufferings, because we know that suffering produces perseverance; perseverance, character; and character, hope. And hope does not disappoint us, because God has poured out his love into our hearts by the Holy Spirit, whom he has given us" (Romans 5:3-4).

3. *He calls me to rejoice in my pain*—"Consider it pure joy, my brothers, whenever you face trials of many kinds, because you know that the testing of your faith develops perseverance. Perseverance must finish its work so that you may be mature and complete, not lacking anything" (James 1:2-4).

4. *He invites me to submit to my faithful Creator*—"Those who suffer according to God's will should commit themselves to their faithful Creator and continue to do good" (1 Peter 4:19).

A small boy was flying a kite high in the sky when it drifted into a cloud bank and disappeared from view. A passerby asked the little boy what he was doing. "I'm flying my kite," the child responded. The man, looking up and seeing only the cloud bank, said, "I don't see any kite. How do you know it's still there?" "I don't see it either," replied the boy, "but I know it's up there because every once in a while there's a tug on my string."

Many Christians feel God has disappeared just when they need Him most. Take heart, child of God. Just because you can't see Him doesn't mean He is not there. Keep holding on to the Lord. He is faithful even when you cannot feel His presence. Hang on, and sooner or later you will feel the "tug on the line" that lets you know He is still there.

The Challenge for Us

I received a letter from a prisoner who had read my book *What a Christian Believes*. He received a free copy through Prison Fellowship and wrote to say thanks. Here is part of his letter:

> Hello, Sir! My name is Brandon and I am currently in prison in Arizona. I have just finished reading your book for the first time about 2½ hours ago. Your book has moved me greatly towards picking up the Bible once again.

> I was raised a Catholic, went to St. Francis of Assisi from first to eighth grade. But as I grew older I lost my way down the road and I am so far lost I don't even know how many miles I will have to backtrack just to find the spot where I detoured at, then start down the proper path again.

> I do not know if I can pick a favorite chapter but I will say that I plan on reading "Did Mickey Mantle Go to Heaven?" over and over because not only do I like what it says, but I need to read it more times than one just to remind me what I am supposed to believe about the forgiveness of sins.

> That is an extremely hard part of my faith to remember. Shoot, just the faith part is hard for me, Mr. Pritchard.

He signed his letter, "Searching for Christ." I believe he is not far from the kingdom. Being in prison is not an easy thing, but it can be good if your prison time leads you to salvation. And I smiled when I read that the "faith part" is hard for him. There are times when the "faith part" is hard for all of us.

How faithful is God? He is so faithful that anyone who seeks Him can find Him. Faith is a gift, but even a gift must be opened to be enjoyed. As we exercise our faith, we begin to discover more and more about God's purpose in our trials. Our challenge is to trust when we cannot see and to hold on to the rope of faith until we feel the tug from heaven that tells us He is there.

CHAPTER 2

His Faithfulness in Every Circumstance

Do all things really work together for good? Consider the following:

- A little baby is born with no brain, only a brain stem. The doctors tell the parents that she has no chance of surviving. Somehow she stays alive for 16 months. The parents struggle to take care of her. When she gets sick, the doctors tell the parents, "Don't bring her to the hospital. There is nothing we can do for her."

- A seemingly healthy 12-year-old girl develops severe migraine headaches. On Friday she is taken to the hospital; on Saturday she dies. Her father said she was "the sunshine of my life."

- A man and a woman meet while attending Bible college, fall in love, and get married. Feeling called to the mission field, they end up serving the Lord in a remote stretch of the Amazon River in north-eastern Peru. While on a routine flight back to their houseboat, the Peruvian Air Force mistakes them for drug smugglers and shoots their plane out of the sky. One bullet rips through the mother and into the head of their infant daughter who was sitting in her lap. Both are killed instantly.

• One day a policeman stops a man known to be a drug dealer. It happens on a busy downtown street and a crowd gathers to watch the unfolding drama. There is a struggle and somehow the drug dealer grabs the officer's gun. Someone in the crowd yells, "Shoot him, man." And he does, at point-blank range, in the face. The officer was in his early twenties.

These stories are all true. The first happened to dear friends in Texas, the second to a well-known political leader, the third to missionaries Jim and Ronni Bowers, the fourth on the streets of Dallas. And there are many others who would have no trouble adding stories of their own.

Yet another story comes from some missionary friends in Africa who sent the following e-mail to their supporters:

The news came swiftly and unexpectedly: Dr. Ologunde was dead. Our 34-year-old Nigerian colleague, who was serving at our sister hospital in Egbe, Nigeria, had been found in his bed. He had last been seen late the night before, caring for patients in his usual, careful way.

Dr. Ologunde was a remarkable man. He had trained in the General Medical Practice residency at Evangel Hospital, and had stayed on as consultant and eventually the director of training. When we began hospital work at Evangel, he carefully considered where he could best be used by God—and agreed to answer a desperate need at Egbe Hospital, in the southwest region of the country.

His decision to work at Egbe was not to be taken lightly, for Dr. Ologunde had sickle cell anemia. In fact, when he first began his medical training in Jos he had an acute sickle crisis requiring intensive care treatment. He quietly suffered in daily pain— and was a role model for how far patients with this disease in Nigeria could go. So the blow of his death came hard—to Egbe and to Jos. Here was our brightest and best, a representative of all that our residency program is about. Here was a role model, a husband-to-be, a source of pride to his family and hope to a town—GONE.

Why? Why do these things happen? And why do they happen to good people, decent people, Christian people?

Understanding God's Providence

There is a Bible doctrine that can help lead us toward some sort of understanding as to why. Though it does not answer every question, at least it provides the only possible foundation for understanding. It is the doctrine of the providence of God. In English, the word *providence* has two parts. It's *pro* and *video* put together, literally meaning "to see before." Though the word itself is not found in most modern translations of the Bible, the concept is certainly biblical. It refers to *God's gracious oversight of the universe.* Every one of those words is important. God's *providence* is one aspect of His grace. *Oversight* means that He directs the course of affairs. The word *universe* tells us that God not only knows the big picture, He also concerns Himself with the tiniest details.

Here are five statements that unfold the meaning of God's providence in more detail:

He upholds all things,

He governs all events,

He directs everything to its appointed end,

He does this all the time and in every circumstance,

He does it always for His own glory.

No Accidents, Only Incidents

The doctrine of God's providence teaches us some important truths: *First, God cares about the tiniest details of life.* Nothing escapes His notice, for He is concerned about the small as well as the big. In fact, with God, there is no big or small. He knows when a sparrow falls and He numbers the hairs on your head. He keeps track of the stars in the skies and the rivers that flow to the oceans. He sets the day of your birth, the day of your death, and He ordains everything that comes to pass in between. *Second, He uses everything and wastes nothing.* There are no accidents with God, only incidents. This includes events that seem to us to be senseless tragedies. *Third, God's ultimate purpose is to shape His children into the image of Jesus Christ* (Romans 8:29). He often uses difficult moments and human tragedies to accomplish that purpose.

Many verses in the Bible teach these truths, including Acts 17:28 ("in him we live and move and have our being"), Colossians 1:17 ("in him all things hold together"), Hebrews 1:3 ("...sustaining all things by his powerful word"), Proverbs 16:9 ("in his heart a man plans his course, but the LORD determines his steps"), and especially Psalm 115:3 ("our God is in heaven; he does whatever pleases him").

The doctrine of God's providence is based on a combination of four of His attributes:

Sovereignty—He is in control

Predestination—He is in charge of how everything turns out

Wisdom—He makes no mistakes

Goodness—He has our best interests at heart

In the words of R.C. Sproul, "God doesn't roll dice." Nothing happens by chance. Ever.

Predestination and Free Will

How can predestination and free will exist side by side? How is it possible for both God to predetermine events and for people to make free choices? This is a question that has baffled and divided Christians for 2000 years. And no matter how we formulate our answer, there will still be an area of mystery that we cannot explain and will never understand this side of heaven. With that in mind, let me share a series of statements that help put this question in its proper perspective.

He is in charge of
> what happens
> when it happens
> how it happens
> why it happens
> and even what happens after it happens.

This is true of
> all events
> in every place
> from the beginning of time.

He does this for
> our good
> and His glory.

He is not the author of sin, yet evil serves His purposes.

He does not violate our free will, yet free will serves His purposes.

We're not supposed to understand all this.

We're simply supposed to believe it.

I hope that clears up any misunderstanding! (Actually this statement—brief though it is—does summarize the Christian position on God's providence as it has been developed over the centuries.)

Providence Illustrated

With that as our background, let's turn to consider the story of Joseph. If you are acquainted with the Bible, you have probably heard his story somewhere along the way. It goes something like this: Because Joseph was the favored son of his father, Jacob, he was the object of envy by his many brothers. One day his brothers threw him into a cistern and conspired to sell him into slavery to some Midianites who happened to be traveling by. Having done that, they then splashed his "coat of many colors" with the blood of a goat in order to make it appear that he had been killed by a wild animal. Then they showed the coat to Jacob, who believed their lie and sorrowfully concluded that Joseph was dead.

From Honor to Dishonor

Meanwhile, Joseph was taken to Egypt by the Midianites. There he was sold again, this time to Potiphar, who was head of pharaoh's security force. Genesis 39 tells us that Joseph gained favor with Potiphar because the Lord was blessing Joseph. Eventually Potiphar put Joseph in charge of his entire household, which included the land, care of the property, and oversight of the other slaves. This was a signal honor for a Hebrew slave.

Because Joseph was competent, confident, and good-looking, Potiphar's wife approached him about having a sexual affair. Joseph refused, pointing out that he could not betray Potiphar and he would not sin against God. The woman persisted, to the point that one day when everyone else was gone, she attempted to pull him down on her bed. Joseph fled from the scene, leaving his cloak behind. The woman was humiliated and accused him of rape. It was a false charge, of course, but Potiphar believed his wife and had Joseph thrown in prison.

From Prison to the Palace

While in prison, Joseph prospered once again and gained the respect of his fellow prisoners and of the guards. This happened because the Lord was with him to bless him. Eventually the pharoah's cupbearer and the baker were thrown in the same prison and Joseph befriended them. One night they both had dreams they could not interpret. But Joseph was able to interpret them with the Lord's help. The dreams came true exactly as Joseph had predicted—the baker was hung but the cupbearer was released. Joseph asked the cupbearer to remember him after he was released, but he didn't.

Two years passed, and pharaoh had a dream that he could not interpret. That's when the cupbearer remembered Joseph's amazing ability to interpret dreams and mentioned it to the pharaoh, who ordered Joseph brought before him. Joseph correctly interpreted the dream and was rewarded by pharaoh, who made him the prime minister of Egypt. Not bad for a Hebrew slave who had been sold into slavery by his brothers!

Eventually a famine settled on the Near East. Jacob told his sons to go to Egypt and buy some grain. They went and, in the process, met Joseph—only they didn't know it was Joseph. This happened twice. Then Joseph revealed his true identity. They were shocked and then scared because they had betrayed him and now he was in a position to get even. But Joseph didn't do that. In fact, he stunned them with these words:

> Do not be distressed and do not be angry with yourselves for selling me here, because it was to save lives that God sent me ahead of you. For two years now there has been famine in the land, and for the next five years there will not be plowing and reaping. But God sent me ahead of you to preserve for you a remnant on earth and to save your lives by a great deliverance. So then, it was not you who sent me here, but God (Genesis 45:5-8).

From Famine to Plenty

And that's not the end of the story. The brothers went back to Canaan and told their aged father that Joseph was still alive. He couldn't believe it, but due to the terrible famine conditions in the land, eventually they convinced him to go to Egypt with them. He made the trip and was reunited with the son he had given up for dead many years ago. Then he met the pharaoh, who offered to let Joseph's family settle in Egypt for as long as they wanted. The family settled in Egypt and lived in peace there for many years. Finally Jacob died at the age of 147. Then it was just Joseph and his brothers. They feared that with Jacob's death, Joseph would be free to take revenge on them. So they told Joseph, "Oh, by the way, before Dad died, he told us to tell you to treat us kindly." It sounds like just one more deceptive attempt to cover their guilt.

Listen to Joseph's response. These are the words of a man who believes in the providence of God:

Don't be afraid. Am I in the place of God? You intended to harm me, but God intended it for good to accomplish what is now being done, the saving of many lives (Genesis 50:19-20).

The New American Standard Bible translates verse 20 this way: "You meant evil against me, but God meant it for good." *Both sides of that statement are true.* "You meant evil against me"—what the brothers had done was indeed evil, and Joseph didn't sugarcoat the truth. They were 100 percent responsible for their sin. "God meant it for good"—this doesn't mean that evil isn't evil. It just means that God is able to take the evil actions of sinful men and to use them to accomplish His plans. Joseph saw the "invisible hand" of God at work in his life. He understood that behind his conniving brothers stood the Lord God, who had orchestrated the entire affair in order to get Joseph to just the right place at just the right moment in order to save his whole family.

At Just the Right Moment

Joseph was saying, "Though your motives were bad, God's motives were good." *And though it took years and years for God's purposes to become clear, in the end, Joseph saw the hand of God behind everything that had happened to him.*

Think about the implications of that statement:

At just the right moment, Joseph's brothers threw him into the cistern.

At just the right moment, the Midianites came along.

At just the right moment, Joseph was sold to Potiphar.

At just the right moment, Potiphar's wife falsely accused him.

At just the right moment, he met the baker and the cupbearer.

At just the right moment, the cupbearer remembered Joseph.

At just the right moment, pharaoh called for Joseph.

At just the right moment, Joseph was promoted to prime minister.

At just the right moment, Jacob sent his sons to Egypt.

At just the right moment, the brothers met Joseph.

At just the right moment, Jacob's family moved to Egypt.

At just the right moment, pharaoh offered Joseph's family the land of Goshen.

At just the right moment, they settled there and prospered.

All of these events happened at "just the right moment" and in "just the right way" so the right people would be in the right place so that in the end everything would come out the way God had ordained in the beginning. *God never violated anyone's free will, yet everything happened as He had planned*. That's the providence of God in action. That's also what Romans 8:28 means when it says that "in all things God works for the good of those who love him, who have been called according to his purpose" (Romans 8:28).

The Results of Trusting God's Providence

If we truly believe in the providence of God, it revolutionizes the way we look at life, especially the unexplainable tragedies that come to all of us sooner or later. Let's consider three implications in particular.

1. Trusting God's providence frees us from bitterness.

This is clearly the message of Genesis 50:20, where Joseph said, "You intended to harm me, but God intended it for good." If ever any man had the right to get even, it was Joseph. We get bitter because we doubt God's goodness and we don't see His invisible hand at work in our lives. We think God isn't involved in our situation and that's why we get angry and try to get even and hurt those who have hurt us. But when you come to believe God is at work in your life, you will find yourself being able to rest in the confidence that He will work out your circumstances for the best. You will feel as if you can just stand back and let God do whatever He wants to do.

2. Trusting God's providence gives us a new perspective on our tragedies.

Consider this: *God is involved with us even in the worst moments of life.* I believe that in the great issues of life, we will generally not have an answer to the question "Why did this happen to me?" That is, we won't know why our mate got sick or why we lost our life savings or why God didn't intervene when we were being sexually abused. Most of the time we are simply left to wonder why these things happened. Who would dare to say to a woman, "This is why your child was stillborn" or to the grieving people of the church in Nigeria, "This is why Dr. Ologunde died so suddenly"?

But it is at this point that trusting God's providence is so crucial. *It doesn't tell us everything we would like to know about the mysteries of life, but it does assure us that God is there and that He cares for us.* He is somehow involved even in our darkest moments in a way we cannot see—and probably wouldn't understand even if we could see it.

Because of God's providence, we can keep believing in God even in the face of many unanswered questions. He can bear the burden of all those questions.

3. *Trusting God's providence gives us the courage to keep going in hard times.*

Because God is there, we know that He cares for us, even when life is tumbling in all around us. One Saturday night a few years ago I was working in my office at home. My office is located in the corner of our basement, which helps ensure I won't be bothered and I won't bother anyone else. I rarely have visitors to my office at home, and no one ever drops by on a Saturday night. But on this particular night, I heard a knock at the door. When I opened it, there stood an old friend with tears streaming down his face. As he walked in and sat down, he kept repeating two words: "It's over." I knew what he meant. His marriage was coming to a very sad end. Although both he and his wife were Christians, a series of sinful choices had brought their marriage to a total collapse. That night she had told him that she was filing for a divorce. My friend sat in my office, tears coursing down his cheeks, thoroughly broken as he realized that soon his marriage would be over and he would be divorced.

He went on to say that two things had sustained him during this agonizing personal crisis. The first one was a song that had been playing on the local Christian station: "Life Is Hard but God Is Good." He had heard it so many times that he knew the words by heart. And he had discovered through his pain that both parts of the title were true.

Life *is* hard. No one had to convince him of that. But as he contemplated the wreckage of a marriage he had hoped would last forever, he was discovering that even in his pain, God *is* good.

Then he said that recently he had learned a verse of Scripture that had helped him greatly. It was Psalm 115:3: "Our God is in heaven; he does whatever pleases him." On the surface that might seem a strange verse for such a sad moment, yet to him it had been a lifeline. *The truth of God's sovereignty meant that what was happening to him was part of the outworking of God's plan.* Though human sin had caused it, God had allowed it to come and He did not intervene to stop it. Therefore, God would help him through it, and in the end, he would learn many painful and much-needed lessons.

Now all of that happened a number of years ago. Looking back, my friend would say that today he believes Psalm 115:3 even more than he did then. Nothing happens anywhere in the universe by accident. There is no such thing as luck or fate or chance. God is at work in all things at all times to accomplish His will. That's God's providence at work. And while trusting His providence doesn't answer every question, doesn't make our problems go away, and doesn't give us an easy road, it *does* tell us that there is a pattern to the seemingly random events taking place in our life, and that God is designing something beautiful out of what now seems to be only a chaos of clashing colors. Life *is* hard—make no mistake about that. But God *is* good. Both those statements are true all the time for all God's children.

Full Confidence in God's Providence

Earlier I quoted the first part of the message from our friends in Nigeria about the death of Dr. Ologunde. Let me now share the last few paragraphs they wrote:

And yet, even in this tragedy, we can rejoice. As one of our physician colleagues pointed out, Dr. Ologunde is not taking pain medication now— nor will he ever again. If given the chance, he himself would not come back, for he is in a far better place. Dr. Ologunde was a man of spiritual maturity and integrity. His faith in Christ was intense and genuine—and a challenge to us. He encouraged a holistic approach to patients that would never neglect the spiritual side of those who come to our hospital.

Can he be replaced? No, of course not. Will God's plan for Egbe Hospital be carried out? Of course. Was it a mistake for Dr. Ologunde to have agreed to serve in that remote location? Never.

We count ourselves privileged to have worked for a short time with this man. It greatly enriched our first months in our medical ministry—and we will miss him.

> With full confidence in the
> resurrection of the saints,
> The Kirschner family in Jos, Nigeria

"With full confidence in the resurrection of the saints." That's the trust of God's providence at work in the worst moments of life. If God is not there as we lay our loved ones into the ground, and if His plans are not being worked out when our loved ones are taken from us, then there is no hope for any of us. But if He is there, then we can face the future "with full confidence."

Life is a mysterious journey, full of unexpected twists and turns. The path ahead is a mystery to us all. No one can say for sure what is around the next bend. It may be a smooth road through a lovely valley, or we may discover that the bridge is washed out and we have to find a way to cross a deep river. Often the road will seem to disappear, or it may suddenly seem to go in three different directions and we won't know which way to go. But there is One who knows the way because the past, present, and future are all the same to Him and the darkness is as the light of day. He knows the way we should go. *And when we get to heaven, we will discover that the Lord was with us even in the darkest moments.* Until that morning comes and the sunlight of God's presence fills our faces, we move on through the twilight still believing that though life is hard, God is good. And in the end as we look back on our earthly pilgrimage, we will say with all the children of God, "Jesus led me all the way."

CHAPTER 3

His Faithfulness to the Suffering

Before I was afflicted I went astray, but now I obey your word (Psalm 119:67).

It was good for me to be afflicted so that I might learn your decrees (Psalm 119:71).

I know, O LORD, that your laws are righteous, and in faithfulness you have afflicted me (Psalm 119:75).

These three verses all use the verb "afflicted," which comes from the noun *affliction,* an old word that speaks of any difficult or painful circumstance. *Afflictions come in all shapes and sizes.* An affliction can be as small as an aggravating head cold or as large as a major illness, the loss of a job, public persecution, or rumors spread by your enemies. Or an affliction could be the sort of cosmic suffering Job experienced. One writer I consulted said that we don't need to seek affliction because sooner or later, it will seek us. I'm sure that's true. Sometimes our troubles come because we are just plain stupid. And we may have big trouble when we are repeatedly stupid. Other times we suffer because we live in a fallen world where disease spreads, babies get sick, terrorists fly planes into skyscrapers, and volcanoes erupt in the Congo. Sometimes we suffer not because we do wrong but because we do right and someone else doesn't like it. Being good isn't a guarantee that you won't have problems.

Here's a verse to consider as we begin this chapter: "Many are the afflictions of the righteous, but the LORD delivers him out of them all" (Psalm 34:19 NASB). Most of us probably like that second part about deliverance, but this chapter is mostly about the first part, the many afflictions the righteous suffer. If you want the message of this chapter in one sentence, here it is: *It's not what happens to us that matters; it's how we respond that makes the difference.* The writer of Psalm 119 had a lot to say about trouble. Evidently he had suffered so much that he had become a sort of expert in the field. His words remind us forcefully that God is intimately involved in our troubles. Nothing happens—no matter how bad it may seem—by accident.

Your Troubles Are Not About You

I've known Steve and Liz Massey for almost 20 years. Steve was an elder of the church I pastored in Texas and Liz often sang solos during our worship services. Their children attended AWANA with our children. Our family lost touch with them when we moved to Oak Park, Illinois in 1989. About nine years ago Steve came through Chicago on business and we ate supper together. I was surprised to learn that he had started writing poetry, and I recalled that he had sent me a poem about my youngest son and one of his friends. Then in 1996 we traveled through Dallas and saw Steve and Liz at a reunion of folks from our old church. That's when I learned that Liz had been having some serious health problems. A few months ago, Steve wrote to say that Liz needed a kidney transplant and that their son Aaron was going to donate one of his kidneys to his mother.

After the operation, Steve sent me a small book of poems he had written called *Plans for You*. At a low point he wrote a poem called "The Author of Miracles" that included these words: "We need a miracle now/ a Band-Aid or aspirin won't do/ 'cause we need a miracle now. Not a walk on water/ or mountain in the sea miracle/ but a healing from you. We've so little faith somehow/ but since all power resides in you/ that's where we'll rest now. Lord, we've just found out/ that we need a miracle now/ so we send up our request and rest in you now."

Evidently the miracle came in one form or another because the surgery was successful even though Liz's body keeps trying to reject Aaron's kidney. The battle continues, the war is not over. In a recent note he commented that trials are difficult mostly because we don't know when (or if) they will end. Then he added this thought: "Liz and I are beginning to appreciate Job. He kept getting sicker and sicker, yet he refused to curse God and die. (I'm working on a spoof piece dedicated to our choir entitled, 'The More You Pray, the Sicker We Get.') Trials are not about time. They are not about double blessings you might get if you endure like Job did. (If Job had bugged out one day early, would he have received anything from God? How many Christians bug out of their college/business/marriage one day early?) Trials are about God. Illness happens because life happens. So you're having a bad year. So! Who's in charge?"

"Trials are about God." What a good thought that is. *Your troubles are not about you. Your troubles are about God.* They are sent to teach you things about God you couldn't learn any other way. With that in mind, let's take a closer look at these three verses from Psalm 119 that appeared at the beginning of this chapter. They give us a panoramic view of how God uses affliction to teach us His Word and to build our faith so we end up closer to Him than we were before our troubles began.

God's Work Through Our Troubles

Before My Troubles: Straying

"Before I was afflicted I went astray, but now I obey your word" (Psalm 119:67).

At first glance this verse may seem to apply only to those who go astray into some sort of obvious moral sin. But the word "astray" simply means to go our own way, like the proverbial sheep of Isaiah 53:6. The psalmist means that before his troubles came, he was on top of the world, tooling down the highway of life with the top down and the music blaring. He was "the most from coast to coast," his life was on cruise control, things were good, his wife was happy, his kids were doing great, his career was on the upswing, and little by little he was reaching his goals. Life wasn't perfect, but it sure was good. He prayed, but not much. He read his Bible, but not with much conviction. He went through the motions, but in his heart he felt pretty good about how things were going. His prosperity had caused him to push God to the edges of his life. But then all of that changed—God had other plans for him.

How often do we consider how thin the line is between joy and sorrow? Just one phone call, and your life could be shattered forever. That's all it takes. Just one phone call, and things will never be the same. Of course we live as if that call will never come. But it could come at any moment. And when it does, our house of cards will come tumbling down. When people ask me, "Do you think God can speak to us today?" I always tell them, "He's got your number and He can ring your phone any time He wants." God can speak to us through our troubles, and He can stop us in our tracks.

I once had the opportunity to spend five days lecturing on the book of Galatians to 600 students at Word of Life Bible Institute in Pottersville, New York. After one of my sessions, a student came up to talk to me. She had a friend who claims to be a Christian but persists in choosing the path of sexual sin. When she talks to her friend and shares God's Word, her friend is always glad to hear the truth and promises to change her ways. But then the friend goes back to her sinful habits. What should she do? I advised the student that besides remaining friends with her, she had one major way to help. *She should pray that God would do whatever it takes to bring her friend to repentance.* If that means hitting rock bottom, then so be it. After all, if you never face the consequences, why stop sinning? Many times I have urged Christians to pray like this for their loved ones who are far from God: "Lord, do whatever it takes. Hold nothing back. If it must be through pain, then let it be through pain that my loved ones may come to their senses and run to the cross of Christ for forgiveness." It is not easy to pray this way, but I am convinced it is entirely biblical. All you are saying is "Do whatever it takes to get their attention." That's a prayer God can answer in many different ways.

C.S. Lewis remarked that God whispers in our pleasure but He shouts in our pain. Pain is God's megaphone to rouse a sleeping world. That's what the psalmist meant in Psalm 119:67. His afflictions roused him and led him back to the Lord. Earlier he had been living for himself, but now he obeys God's Word.

During My Troubles: Learning

"It was good for me to be afflicted so that I might learn your decrees" (Psalm 119:71).

Most of us would have a hard time saying, "It was good for me to be afflicted." By definition, affliction is painful to endure. How could we ever call it good? Yet that is exactly what the psalmist said about his own suffering. I suppose that most modern Christians would rather identify with Peter on the Mount of Transfiguration when, after seeing Jesus standing alongside Moses and Elijah, he declared, "It is good

for us to be here." Then he volunteered to build three taber-
nacles so they could stay there for a while and have a personal Bible conference. Sure, why not? Sounds like a fine
idea to me. There is nothing wrong with being on the mountaintop. We all need those experiences occasionally, and no
doubt we would like to stay on the mountaintop if we could.
I smile when I consider Luke's parenthetical observation on
Peter's comment: "He did not know what he was saying"
(Luke 9:33). *Sooner or later we all have to go back down into
the valley.* The mountaintop is a good break from the routine of life, but it doesn't last forever. You have to go back
into the world of pain and suffering, where bad things
happen to good people and where life isn't neat or easy or
always fun. If your God is only a "God of the good times"
or a "God of the mountaintops," then your God is not the
God of the Bible. The true God is often best seen in the
darkness and His presence most powerfully felt in times of
deepest sorrow.

*One of the purposes of affliction is to teach us things we
would not otherwise know.* Until hard times come, our
knowledge of God and His Word tends to be rather theoretical, like the knowledge of the man who reads three
books on car repair and then opens an auto repair shop.
When my car breaks down, I want a man with some grease
under his fingernails. If he's too clean, or if he looks like he's
just come from the library, I worry that maybe he doesn't
have enough experience. Give me a man who knows, by
experience, the difference between a fuel pump and a water
pump.

Our Best Schoolmaster

*The psalmist declared that passing through the valley of
sorrow was good for him because through it all, he learned
the Word of God.* Martin Luther commented that he never
learned the Word until he was afflicted. His sufferings were

his best schoolmasters. This is a hard reality for many Christians to face because we don't like dealing with negative circumstances. Perhaps we would prefer that our marriage be different, or our career move in a different direction, or our finances improve, or our health change for the better. No doubt most of us would change certain things about our own situation if we were in charge of the universe. But can we be certain that our choices would be better than God's? Just because you don't like your situation doesn't mean you don't need to be there. Your personal satisfaction with life is not necessarily a good gauge of where you need to be right now.

When we factor God into the equation, things look very different. It's not that the affliction itself is less painful or that something sad has been made happy or that evil has somehow become good. And it doesn't mean that you would not change things if you could. When we bring God into the equation, we look back and see how it was good for us to go through hard times because we learned truths about God and ourselves that we would never have known otherwise. About God, we learn that His ways are far beyond our ways, that He is holy and righteous and full of mercy, and that He is always faithful to His children. About ourselves, we learn that we aren't as strong or as wise or as powerful or as clever as we thought we were. In the end, we are exposed as helpless children desperately in need of our heavenly Father.

You Can't Rush God

As I look back over more than 30 years as a Christian, I can testify that the greatest times of personal growth have come during the times of greatest sorrow and disappointment. In November of 1974 my father died—just three months after Marlene and I were married. The world I had known disappeared the day he died and another world took its place. Things have never gone back to what they used to be. Fourteen years later I lost my job and for a while had no way to support my family. For months I felt suspended in midair, with no clear direction for the future and not much money to pay the bills. I remember vividly that my friend Rick Suddith told me that things weren't likely to change anytime soon and I should get a rocking chair, go sit on my front porch, and think about life and let God speak to me. I learned the hard way the truth of four simple words: "You can't rush God." *He won't be pushed and He doesn't take kindly to those who try to rush Him.* As I look back on those experiences, I am aware that God worked in my life to produce needed change and to prod me to greater growth. I can truly testify that it has been good for me to be afflicted in order that God might do His work in my life.

All too often our prayers in times of difficulty boil down to three words: "Change my circumstances." While praying like that isn't wrong, it can lead us in a wrong direction. If we take Psalm 119 seriously, we ought instead to pray, "Lord, teach me your Word." Instead, we say, "Lord, change my marriage or get me out of it." "Change my boss so she will appreciate me." "Change my health so I will feel better." "Change my financial condition so I can pay my bills." Who among us hasn't prayed along those lines? But consider this: Perhaps God has not changed your circumstances because He first wants to change you.

Over the last few months I've been repeatedly impressed with certain themes that recur in the Old and New Testaments. I am struck by how often God says, "Wait" in the Old Testament. Psalm 27:14 is just one example: "Wait for the LORD; be strong and take heart and wait for the LORD." And in the New Testament I am struck by how often Paul prays that his readers might have grace to endure and persevere. This comes out clearly in Colossians 1:11, where Paul prays that his readers might be "strengthened with all power according to his glorious might so that you may have great endurance and patience." Often when we want things to change, God's word to us is "wait," "endure," "be patient," and "persevere." Which is why long-suffering is a fruit of the Spirit (Galatians 5:22 KJV). When it comes to this virtue, we would prefer that God give us *short*-suffering, but of course, that's not on the heavenly menu. It is as we wait and endure and persevere that we learn God's Word, grow in grace, and learn that which we never knew before. Only then can we look back and say, "As hard as it was, and although I didn't expect it or want it and even now I might wish things had worked out some other way, I stand and declare that my God is faithful in all things. I see now that it was good for me to pass through the fire of affliction, and I praise God for His wise plan for my life."

After My Troubles: Knowing

"I know, O Lord, that your laws are righteous, and in faithfulness you have afflicted me" (Psalm 119:75).

The phrase "I know" speaks of settled knowledge—the kind that comes only by looking back over the years and seeing again and again how God has helped you in times of heartache and trouble. Most of us know that little poem called "Footprints," about the two sets of footprints in the sand, one set being yours, and the other set belonging to the Lord, who walked with you. But during the darkest moments, we see only one set of prints in the sand. Why? "My child, when you couldn't walk, I carried you in My arms," says the Lord. The poem is so popular because it speaks to a near-universal experience. *As we look back, we can see times that were so difficult that we know deep in our souls if God had not carried us, we would not have made it through.* That's the sort of tested knowledge the psalmist is talking about in Psalm 119:75.

The psalmist declares that he now knows three things as a result of his afflictions:

- Everything God says is right.

- God is faithful even in our troubles.

- He is involved in everything that happens to us.

When times are tough, it's easy to conclude, "Lord, this must be a mistake." But consider how the psalmist puts it: "In faithfulness you have afflicted me." Somehow he sees beyond his current misery, past the pain of difficult circumstances, and through the fog of many unanswered questions to apprehend the hand of a loving and faithful God who is working in, with, and through his troubles to accomplish His divine purposes. *What a high view of sovereignty this is!* Even the attacks of the psalmist's enemies cannot happen apart from God's gracious permission. Not even Satan himself can touch him unless God wills it so. No weapon formed against him can prosper, and any evil weapon that touches him must be allowed to do so—not in spite of God's faithfulness, but because of it.

The Greatest of God's Sovereignty

This is the very highest level of faith. *To think like this means that you come to the conclusion that God is so sovereign that nothing can happen to you that He has not planned for His glory and your ultimate benefit.* I am reminded of Jim Bowers' comment after the death of his wife Roni and their infant daughter Charity when their missionary airplane was blown out of the sky by a Peruvian jet in April 2001. Humanly speaking, it was a tragedy that should never have happened. Of the many bullets that sprayed the tiny plane, one single bullet took the life of his wife and his daughter. Looking back, Jim Bowers called it a "sovereign bullet." Only a man who knows God can say a thing like that. But that is exactly the sort of thing the psalmist is saying in Psalm 119:75. As he looks back over his life, the good times and the bad, the happy days and the sad nights, he knows that all that has happened to him is not by chance or fate or some sort of cosmic roulette. It has come to him as proof of God's faithfulness to His children. So far from shattering his faith, in the end, his troubles have strengthened his faith. When I heard Jim Bowers speak at Moody Founders Week, he declared his total faith in God's sovereignty in the death of his wife and daughter. "Nothing bad happened to them," he said. "They got to heaven quicker than we did." Is that faith or fantasy talking? I submit that those are the words of a man of faith who, out of great personal loss, has rested his faith in the promises of God. Even the worst tragedy doesn't appear as such when viewed from heaven's perspective.

Oh, for a faith like that!

I should add that this sort of faith has enormous evangelistic power. The world stands in awe of a suffering saint who clings to his faith in the midst of horrific circumstances. *The world can partially counterfeit our joy, but it has no answer for the faith that shines the brightest in the darkest hours of the night.* When the world sees our faith rising above and beyond our circumstances, it asks, "From whence does this come?" And then the door is open to talk about how Jesus Christ has changed everything for us.

Our Response: Three Stages of Faith

As we wrap up this chapter, let's consider the stages of faith during affliction:

First, there is faith that *obeys:* "Now I keep your Word."

Second, there is faith that *affirms:* "It is good for me to be afflicted."

Third, there is faith that *glorifies:* "In faithfulness you afflicted me."

When we reach this level, we are really saying, "I would not change it if I could." Not all of us will come to that point, and perhaps we don't have to. Faith must find its own level in each heart. But it is wonderful to look back and declare that God has been proved correct in all that He has done, that things had to happen the way they did, and that in the end, God has glorified Himself even in our sorest trials.

Your troubles are not about you, they're about God! *Your trials are meant to lift your face from earth to heaven that you might discover the riches of divine grace in the hardest moments of life.* This means that your pain is never wasted, even though it may seem that way right now. Everything has a purpose in life, and that purpose is to glorify God and to bring us into a closer walk with Him.

Our Response: Five Simple Suggestions

In light of all of this, how should we respond to the trials, troubles, and afflictions of life? Here are five simple suggestions:

1. Thank God for your troubles.

"In everything give thanks." This we learn in 1 Thessalonians 5:18 (NASB). It is God's will that we should give thanks in every situation. While this does not mean that we must give thanks for everything, it does mean that there are always reasons for gratitude no matter how grim our circumstances might seem. To paraphrase a familiar hymn:

> When upon life's billows, you are tempest-tossed,
> When you are discouraged, thinking all is lost,
> Count your many troubles, name them one by one,
> And it will surprise you what the Lord has done.

It's good and necessary that we "count our blessings." And there is something faith-building about counting your troubles one by one. As you do the counting, you will be surprised to see (if you look carefully) how God has been at work bringing blessings through the troubles of life. Count your troubles, and soon you will be counting your blessings, too.

2. Look for God's fingerprints in your life.

If what I have said is true, then we ought to see evidence of God's work in all the troubles of life. Think of how your troubles have drawn you closer to God. Look for evidence of answered prayer. See if you can't find the work of holy angels on your behalf. God always leaves His fingerprints on everything He touches. Ask God to open your eyes to see how He has worked on your behalf.

3. Immerse yourself in God's Word.

When you are tempted to run from the Word, run to it instead! Jump into the Bible. Read it more, not less. Let your troubles drive you deeper into the Word. If you can't read a whole book, read a chapter. If not a chapter, then just a few verses. Or just one verse. Read it. Pray over it. Cling to it. Recite God's promises back to Him. Let His Word be the foundation of your prayers. *Determine to obey the Word no matter what happens to you or around you.* If you do that, you will emerge from your troubles with a faith much stronger than before your troubles started.

4. Have faith in God.

Don't give up. Don't give in. Tell the Lord that you will continue to believe Him no matter what happens. "Though he slay me, yet will I trust him" (Job 13:15 KJV). Let your friends know that your faith in God has not wavered. Tell the world that you believe God has led you to this place and that He will not desert you now.

5. When your learning becomes knowing, share what you've learned about God with someone else.

One reason God helps us in our times of trouble is so that when we have come through them, we will be equipped to help others in their times of trouble. *God comforts us that we might comfort others.* You might find it helpful to keep a journal that records the ups and downs of life. That sort of written record will remind you of all you went through and how God helped you in your struggles. And it will serve as a written record that you can use to help others in the future.

God at Work

So let me ask you a personal question: *What is your trouble?* Do you find yourself in a difficult place right now? Are there circumstances in your life that you desperately want to change? Are you struggling to keep your faith intact as life seems to tumble in around you? I wish I could tell you that your experience is unusual, but it isn't. The old adage is true: "Into each life some rain must fall." And some people seem to get a continual thunderstorm that turns into a torrential downpour. If life is good for you right now, enjoy it and give thanks to God. It won't stay that way forever. There is trouble around the corner sooner or later...probably sooner.

We're all in the same boat, aren't we? In the movie *Black Hawk Down* is a scene that makes this point. A vehicle filled with wounded American soldiers has come to a stop in the middle of a street where Somali bullets are flying in every direction. The officer in charge tells a soldier to get in and start driving. "I can't," the soldier says, "I'm shot." "We're all shot," the officer replies. "Get in and drive." That little scene resonates because it's so true. We're all wounded in one way or another. And that brings us back to the central truth: *It's not what happens to us that matters. It's how we respond that makes all the difference.* Our troubles are no mistake. In a deep and profound sense, and in a way that we won't fully understand until we get to heaven, our troubles are a gift from God. They humble us, kill our pride, force us to admit our weakness, and drive us to the Savior who alone can help us when all earthly aids have failed.

Sometimes we will face things for which there is no earthly explanation. In those moments we need to erect a sign that reads, "Quiet: God at Work." Meanwhile, hold on, child of God. Keep believing. Don't quit. Don't give up. Let God do His work in you. The greatest tragedy is to miss what God wants to teach us through our troubles. May God bring us to the place where we can say with the psalmist, "It was good for me to be afflicted that I might learn your decrees."

CHAPTER 4

His Faithfulness to the Defeated

The year was 1866. In a log cabin in the little town of Franklin, Kentucky, Thomas Obadiah Chisholm was born. Although he never went to high school or college, he became an elementary school teacher at age 16. Five years later he was named associate editor of the *Franklin Favorite*, the local newspaper. When he was 27, he attended a revival service led by Dr. H.C. Morrison and gave his heart to Christ. In the years following he served as a Methodist minister and later as an insurance agent. He lived for a time in Winona Lake, Indiana, and later in Vineland, New Jersey.

During his lifetime he wrote over 1200 poems. In 1923 he sent a batch of poems to William Runyan, a musician serving at Moody Bible Institute in Chicago. Mr. Runyan was so impressed by one poem in particular that he decided to set it to music. He published it privately, little knowing that it would become one of the most beloved hymns of the twentieth century. It became a favorite of Dr. Will Houghton, president of the Institute, and later became known as the school's unofficial theme song. In 1954 George Beverly Shea introduced it to Great Britain during the Billy Graham crusade at Harringay Arena in London.

Writing in 1941, Thomas Obadiah Chisholm penned these words of personal testimony:

> My income has not been large at any time due to impaired health in the earlier years which has followed me until now. Although I must not fail to record here the unfailing faithfulness of a covenant-keeping God and that he has given me many wonderful displays of his providing care, for which I am filled with astonishing gratefulness.

I love that phrase—"astonishing gratefulness." *Such should be the testimony of every child of God.* The hymn he wrote is based on our text. Most of us know the words by heart. He called it simply "Great Is Thy Faithfulness."[1]

There is something of a paradox in the way we use this hymn. We tend to sing it at moments when we have experienced God's blessings. We sing it at weddings, graduations, and at the end of a year as we look back and see how God's hand led us day by day. Yet this beloved hymn, which has so encouraged God's people, is based on a text written during Israel's lowest moment. If you know what the word *lament* means, you know what the book of Lamentations is all about. Written by Jeremiah as he sat amid the ashes of a destroyed Jerusalem, his mood is bleak, his words dark and angry. His tone is one of near-total despair. For most of the book, there is not one word of hope, not one ray of light.

Then we come to Lamentations 3, and the light begins to break through. It is as if Jeremiah had reached the absolute bottom, then looked up to find himself seeing the face of God. This is what he says: "Because of the LORD's great love we are not consumed, for his compassions never fail. They are new every morning; great is your faithfulness" (Lamentations 3:22-23). In today's world we hear a great deal

---

1. Kenneth W. Osbeck, *101 Hymn Stories* (Grand Rapids: Kregel Publications, 1982), pp. 84-85.

about self-esteem, finding inner strength, and unleashing the "inner champion" who is inside all of us, waiting to be set free. Despite whatever truth may lie in that direction (and I am sure there is some truth there, somewhere), those approaches ultimately fail because they suggest that the answer to every problem is inside us, and if we can just get in touch with our own natural powers, we can scale the heights and defeat every foe. That's probably true when it comes to problems like losing weight or learning how to speak French, but it doesn't have great relevance when your country has been invaded and everything around you lies in ruins. When we face the truly great issues of life, we must eventually admit that our own resources simply are not enough. We are not wise enough, or strong enough, or persuasive enough, or clever enough to face the trials of life in our own strength. We need an answer that comes from somewhere outside of us. We need an answer that comes from God. And it is at this point that the ancient words of Jeremiah speak so powerfully to us in the twenty-first century. When all was lost, the prophet found strength in God.

Hope When All Seems Hopeless

What a challenge this is to all of us! It is one thing to sing "Great Is Thy Faithfulness" at your wedding. It's something else to sing it when your husband announces he is leaving you for another woman. We all sing it when our children graduate from high school. It is more difficult to sing when they are killed by a drunk driver. We gladly sing when the operation is a success. Do we also sing when we bury a loved one because the cancer treatments didn't work?

These two verses in Lamentations are not an answer to the mysteries of life. They do not instruct us about politics or the circumstances we face every day. And we do not find here a detailed statement about intricate theology. It is rather a word about the Lord. *It is a word that declares He is our hope in the midst of hopelessness.* He is our light when all around is darkness. He is the way when we can find no way. He is our reason for living when we would rather give up.

Lamentations 3:22-23 contains four phrases. Each one raises and answers an important question we need to consider.

1. *Why doesn't God destroy me?*

This is not a theoretical question. We all walk closer to the edge than we think. There is a thin line between prosperity and disaster, joy and sorrow, laughter and tears, life and death.

Let a car swerve in front of you.

Let the bullet come three inches lower.

Let the horse stumble.

Let a tiny switch malfunction, causing the whole plane to crash.

Let the train jump the tracks.

Let the brakes give way.

Let a stray germ enter our system.

Let the lightning flash and in a moment we are gone.

Who can understand the mysteries of the universe? Why are you alive today while someone else is dead? Why is it that we have been to many funerals and yet no one has been to ours...yet!

Hear the answer of Jeremiah: "Because of the LORD's great love we are not consumed" (Lamentations 3:22).

Why doesn't God destroy us? He could and He should. He could because He is God and He should because we are sinners.

Why doesn't He? Because "of the LORD's great love." The Hebrew word for "love" is *hesed*, a word rich with meaning. It has within it the idea of "loyal love," of love that will not let go because it does not depend on emotion but on an act of the will. *God loves us because He promised to love us, and nothing can cause Him to break His promise.* Which leads me to say this: *As bad as things are, if it weren't for God, things would be much worse.* That seems obvious, and perhaps it is, but we need to hear it again. If it weren't for God and for His love, no matter how bad things are in your life right now, they would be much worse without the Lord.

We tend to forget that. Many of us go through life with a sense of entitlement. "I deserve this. I've earned it." Even when we pray we think, *I've been good, so God has to do this for me.* How little we understand about God's grace!

Learning About God's Grace

In 1996, James van Tholen became pastor of a Christian Reformed Church in Rochester, New York. Two years later he was diagnosed with a form of cancer that slowly spread through his body. The doctors told him that they could not cure him and that he probably did not have long to live.

What do you say to your congregation in a moment like that? After taking time off for chemotherapy, James returned to his pulpit and preached a sermon called "Surprised by Death" (printed in the May 24, 1999 issue of *Christianity Today*). He remarked that for the first time in his life, he felt as if he had begun to understand God's grace. He wasn't afraid of dying per se, but he now realized, at the age of 33, that he wasn't going to live to be 40 or 50 or 60 or 70. He might live a few more weeks or months, but without a miracle of God, he wouldn't live much longer than that. That's when it hit him. For years he had subconsciously expected to live to a ripe old age. And that meant he had plenty of time to improve himself, to get rid of bad habits, to repair broken relationships, to grow in grace. Now for the first time he realized he didn't have enough time to do it. He would have to go out into eternity less than he wanted to be—with some habits unchanged, some relationships unrepaired, some spiritual growth not accomplished.

It was also at this time that he realized he would have to depend completely on the grace of God. Not just theoretically, but practically and totally. If God's grace wasn't enough, then he was in trouble because there wasn't enough time for massive self-improvement. Romans 5:6-8 became precious to him because it speaks of Christ dying for us while we were "yet" sinners. Our salvation hangs on that little word "yet." Not just that we were sinners once upon a time, but that in some profound way, even though we are saved, we are still sinners desperately in need of grace.

He also said he realized that after he died, he would eventually be forgotten. Not completely, and not by everybody, and not immediately, but life does go on. His friends would have their reunions, in five or ten or 20 years, and he wouldn't be there. Or if he was mentioned at all, it would be brief and in passing. The church would call another minister. We are, he said, like the flowers of the field. We appear for awhile, then the wind comes, the flowers disappear, and in the words of Psalm 103:16, "its place remembers it no more."

In recent years I've done my share of walking through cemeteries. Part of it is a professional interest. As a pastor, I am frequently asked to hold graveside services for the deceased. If I have a few spare moments, I'll walk up and down the rows, reading the various headstones. Not far from where I live there is a graveyard with the remains of many notable people. The great evangelist Billy Sunday is buried there. A Civil War general is there. The parents of Ernest Hemingway are there. There is a large monument in honor of the Haymarket rioters, who are buried there. And then there are thousands of graves of those who were never famous in this life. The inscriptions read "Faithful father," "Beloved mother," "Asleep in Jesus," and "Never forgotten." But some of the graves are so old that it seems unlikely that anyone remembers who is buried there. And that was Pastor van Tholen's point. If we are looking for meaning and significance in our legacy, we're looking in the wrong place. We live, we die, we're buried, and someone else lives in the house we lived in, and for all we know, someone else may drive our car or even wear our clothes.

What is the ground of our Christian hope in the face of death? It is God Himself. Our hope lies in the fact that God's grace reaches us while we are sinners, saves us as sinners, keeps us even when we fail and fail again, and when we die, that same grace takes us all the way to heaven. That truth is the very heart of the Christian gospel.

Understanding God's Grace

While flipping through the TV channels recently, I happened upon C-SPAN and listened as a most agreeable high school teacher from North Dakota said a most foolish thing. Attempting to defend religion, he said that all religions boil down to the Golden Rule: Do unto others as you would have them do unto you. That sounds nice, but is it true? Behind the Golden Rule stands a greater truth: *We are to do unto others as God has done unto us.* Everything starts with God, not with us. God took the initiative to show grace to us even when we were undeserving of it, and we in turn ought to show grace to others.

In many ways, the doctrine of God's grace is one of the hardest to believe. Even in the church we struggle to believe it. One day C.S. Lewis happened to pass by a group discussing which feature of Christianity most separated it from other religions. Without batting an eye, he responded, "Why, grace of course." He is right, of course.

As I mentioned earlier, in one of my books I've written the story of Mickey Mantle's death from liver cancer. When asked about the story during a radio interview, I told how Bobby Richardson and his wife visited Mickey in his hospital room in Dallas just before he died. Mickey gave a clear statement of his faith in Christ and quoted John 3:16 as the basis of his faith. I added that I believe Mickey Mantle is in heaven, not because of his baseball exploits or because of the charitable work he did, but because before he died he trusted in Jesus Christ.

"So you believe a person can be saved at the end of his life?" I was asked.

"Sure. Look at the thief on the cross," I replied.

Then the interviewer asked a question I wasn't prepared to answer: "What about Jeffrey Dahmer?" According to press reports, he claimed to accept Christ before his death in prison. Could a serial murderer/sexual abuser/cannibal be saved? My answer went something like this: "We like to think that some people are so bad they are beyond God's grace—that God saves moderately bad people who are slightly less than perfect, but the really bad cases He sends straight to hell. I don't know about Jeffrey Dahmer's soul. That's for God alone to know. But I know this much about salvation: It's either all of grace or not of grace at all. And nothing in between."

Do you want mercy or justice? If justice, you'll have it and be sorry for it. If mercy, then you can have it, but just remember when you receive it, you don't deserve it. Life itself is a gift from God.

2. How do I know God will keep on loving me?

"For his compassions never fail" (Lamentations 3:22). The best part of this little phrase is the word "compassions." Note that it's plural. That's very unusual in English. When I entered this verse in my word processor, the spellchecker didn't like it and kicked the word out. So I added it to the dictionary. God's compassion is plural. It comes in waves rolling down from heaven. James 4:6 says, "He gives us more grace," and John 1:16 speaks of "one blessing after another."

I mentioned earlier that many of us have a well-developed sense of entitlement. Along the way we have lost a sense of gratitude for our blessings. I think that's especially true regarding the simple blessings we receive every day. In the words of the crusty curmudgeon Andy Rooney, "For most of life, nothing wonderful happens." He goes on to say that if you can't find happiness in things like having a cup of coffee with your wife or sitting down to a meal with family and friends, then you're probably not going to be very happy. If you sit around dreaming about winning the big contract or hoping for the love of your life to call you up or wondering when the Yankees are going to make you their starting pitcher, you're going to spend most of your days waiting for something that isn't going to happen.

Meanwhile, the sun will rise tomorrow and you won't see it. A friend will say hello and it won't matter, your children will giggle but you won't smile, the roses will bloom, white snow will cover the front yard, your husband will offer to rub your back, the choir will sing your favorite hymn, and because it's ordinary or you've seen it before or heard it before or done it before and because you're dreaming of the future, you'll miss it altogether.

How blessed we already are...and how easy it is to forget what God has done for us. Not long ago a fine-looking young couple came to see me. I didn't know them and didn't know much about their problem. After some discussion the issue was out on the table. It's a genuine problem, but it's not the end of the world. With some grace and patience it could be solved or at least circumnavigated. At one point I looked at the husband and saw his face contorted in a way that said, "I'm not happy about this." So I asked, "What do you think?" "It's fine with me," he said, which meant, "It's not fine with me."

So we talked some more. Things weren't perfect in their marriage and he wasn't happy. Eventually it came out that he had had cancer but had been cured. At that point I did something I can't remember ever doing before. I stood up and looked at both of them across my desk. Raising my voice, I addressed the husband. "I spend my days talking with the sick and dying. I bury people every year who die of cancer. Look at you. You've got a lovely wife, a good marriage, wonderful children; you've both got good jobs and a great future ahead of you. And you've been cured of cancer. Half the people in my church either have cancer or know someone who has it and they are praying for a loved one to be cured. You are one of the fortunate ones; you've beaten the odds. Now you're unhappy because things aren't perfect. You ought to be down on your knees every morning thanking God for all your blessings. God has been so good to you that you shouldn't complain again, ever."

He smiled sheepishly and agreed with me. How blessed we already are! If only we would open our eyes to see what God has done for us. His compassions never fail.

3. When will God give me what I need?

"They are new every morning" (Lamentations 3:23). Here is a word of hope for fearful saints. God's mercies are brand new every morning. The experience of the children of Israel in the Sinai wilderness provides a powerful illustration of this principle. Exodus 16 records the story. The Israelites had

just crossed the Red Sea. After that great miracle, they started grumbling. They were out in the middle of the desert saying, "Why did you bring us out here? At least we had food back in Egypt. Who cares about miracles? We're going to starve to death." So Moses went to God and said, "God, I've got trouble with Your people." And God said, "You think you've got problems? I've got problems. Tell them to get ready because I am going to provide food for them." So the Lord sent the children of Israel manna and quail. The quail were going to come flying in low to the ground at night. The next morning the Jews would find dew on the ground and when the dew disappeared, they would find wafers that tasted like crackers with honey—manna.

Now, God's instructions were very specific: "Go out and get as much as you need for yourself and your family. But don't get any more than you need." Why? Because if you get any more than you need, it will rot and the maggots will infest your manna. God added, "On the day before the Sabbath you can collect for two days, but that's it. Anyone who tries to hoard extra manna will end up with a worm-infested, rotting mess." I'm sure if I had been there I would have sent my three sons out with the wheelbarrow that first week and told them, "Put some under the bed. You never know, this may not show up tomorrow." I think I would have been on the wormy side of things for a couple of weeks just trying to play it safe. God gave His people manna day by day to teach them to trust Him one day at a time.

Consider what this means:

- *We never have to live on yesterday's blessings.* They are new every morning.

- *God's blessings are never early, but they aren't late, either.* They are new every morning.

Today's mercies are for today's burdens. Tomorrow's mercies will be for tomorrow's problems. Somewhere I read about Winston Churchill and his personal struggles during a hard period when he was prime minister of Great Britain. Hoping to console him, his wife suggested that his trouble was really a blessing in disguise. "If so, it is very well disguised," he replied. Many of us no doubt feel the same way about our own problems. We see the trouble, but where is the blessing?

We frequently wonder what will happen tomorrow. Will our health hold up, or will we have a heart attack or a sudden stroke? Will we end up in a nursing home, or waste away in a hospital? What about our children? Will they serve the Lord? What if something happens to them? Who will take care of us in our old age? Singles wonder if they will ever marry. Married couples look at all the divorces and wonder if they will make it. We all have concerns about our career choices and we wonder where we will be in ten years. Just yesterday I got an e-mail from some old friends who are facing a career change. They asked for prayer because the future seems very uncertain. Let us learn the lesson of Lamentations 3:23: God's mercies come day by day. They come when we need them—not earlier and not later. God gives us what we need today. If we needed more, He would give us more. When we need something else, He will give that as well. Nothing we truly need will ever be withheld from us. Search your problems, and within them you will discover the well-disguised mercies of God.

4. *What is my hope for the future?*

"Great is your faithfulness" (Lamentations 3:23). This is the text that led Thomas Obadiah Chisholm to write the poem that became a beloved hymn sung on every continent. Here's a simple way to bring its truth into focus: Great is our *fickleness*...great is Thy *faithfulness*.

We may grow weary...but our God cannot.

We may give up...but our God cannot.

We may fluctuate...but our God cannot.

We may vacillate...but our God cannot.

We may disappoint ourselves...but our God cannot disappoint anyone.

We may fail a thousand times...but our God cannot fail, not even once.

God's faithfulness is so great that we may rest assured that when we come to the final bend in the road, He will be there as we make the journey from earth to heaven. Carrie Enstrom gave me a copy of a letter her father wrote just before his death at the age of 89. Knowing that he was dying of lung cancer, he wrote his grandson (and his grandson's wife) about his own faith in Christ. With Carrie's permission, here is part of what he wrote.

Dear Jeff and Becka,

I hope I can come up with something readable, as I hunt and peck and discover and land on it, as I have fun with my toy, a portable electric typewriter, which I had some of my neighbors get for me at the flea market. It's in like-new condition, but it needs a new ribbon, so until I get one I have to use all capitals.

While I have difficulty with my breathing if I try to move about, I feel fine and have no pain if I sit still and behave myself.... We are so thankful to the Lord, as we look back and see how He has led us to make decisions, do things and make moves that have prepared us for these times that He knew were ahead of us. So each day He gives a fresh taste of His love as He provides.

We hear from your Dad that things are going well for you folks and that you plan to break ground on your new home in the spring. We are so glad for you. I am looking forward to a new home too. It is paid for and debt free, and there will be no maintenance expenses because it is going to last forever. Jesus told His disciples when He was here on earth that I go to prepare a place for you that where I am there ye may be also. I have believed and trusted in the Lord Jesus as my Savior most of my life. It has been such a joy to rejoice with Him in the high smooth times of my life, and to be assured and experience that He was there and helped me in the valleys and rough places.

Have a very happy birthday. We love you so very much, and you are remembered in our prayers.

Love, Grandpa

Not long after writing those words, Carrie's father went to his new home in heaven. I am struck by one phrase in particular: "Each day He gives a fresh taste of His love." Think about that. Each day, we experience God's love and when we die, we go home to heaven.

Can you say that? Do you know that? Is that your personal experience? When your funeral finally comes and some pastor is talking about you, will it be obvious to everyone that you knew Jesus Christ? Or will it be said that you lived for something else? This is our hope for the future—that our God is faithful. We can trust Him today, tomorrow, and forever.

God's Faithfulness Is All We Need

Let's review the four questions and see God's answers:

1. Why doesn't God destroy me?
   "Because of the LORD*'s great love we are not consumed."*

2. How do I know God will keep on loving me?
   "For his compassions never fail."

3. When will God give me what I need?
   "They are new every morning."

4. What is my hope for the future?
   "Great is your faithfulness."

I'd like to share one more word from C.S. Lewis: "He who has God and many other things has no more than he who has God alone." Most of us have many other things. We have money and security and friends and family. But do you also have God in your life? If you do, then the many other things don't matter one way or the other. If you have God, and if you know Jesus Christ, you have enough...because our God is faithful.

CHAPTER 5

His Faithfulness
to the Sick

Is any one of you sick? He should call the elders
of the church to pray over him and anoint him
with oil in the name of the Lord. And the prayer
offered in faith will make the sick person well; the
Lord will raise him up. If he has sinned, he will be
forgiven (James 5:14-15).

P raying for the sick is something we are all asked to do
from time to time. It is certainly something that all
pastors do every week. That fact alone makes the
subject important, especially when I consider that in four
years of seminary, I learned Greek, Hebrew, exegesis,
hermeneutics, theology, and church history, but less than an
hour was spent on this topic.

My own interest in this subject goes back to the fact that
I grew up in a doctor's home. My father was a surgeon and
my mother was an army nurse (they met while doing medical service in the army during World War II). My uncle was
a surgeon and my three brothers are all medical doctors. I
have two cousins who are medical doctors. Medicine hangs
from every branch of my family tree, which is part of the
reason I find the topic of praying for the sick so fascinating.

At what point do medicine and prayer intersect? How should they work together to provide healing?

Let me state up front what the question is *not:*

- The question is not, Does God answer prayer? The answer is yes.

- The question is not, Does God answer prayer for the sick? The answer is also yes.

- The question is not, Does God sometimes answer in ways that seem miraculous? Again, the answer is yes. I am happy to stipulate that all those things are true.

Furthermore, the focus is not on what God can do. After all, we know that God can do anything He wants to do. Nothing is impossible with Him. *Our focus in this chapter is on what the church can do.* I believe James 5:13-16 tells us how a Bible-believing church ought to respond to sickness in its midst. What should we do for the sick? The answer is simple and profound. The church should pray for the sick that God would raise them up. And this ministry of praying for the sick is a crucial part of understanding God's faithfulness.

To say that the church should pray for the sick in its midst is to be faithful to the meaning of the text. However, it also raises a number of valid questions. So that we might have a proper perspective, let's start by considering a few preliminary facts.

A Place to Begin

The Gospels record 41 separate healing miracles during Christ's ministry on earth. Matthew 4:23-24 tells us that people with various maladies were brought to Jesus from

Galilee and Syria, and He healed them all. Some were blind, others deaf, some were demonized, some paralyzed, and still others were sick with various diseases. He healed them all. There is no record of Jesus ever failing to heal anyone who was brought to Him. This means that the total number of healing miracles must be far larger than the 41 specifically mentioned.

As we move into the book of Acts, the situation changes. Some miracles of healing are recorded, but not very many. We read about Peter and John and the lame man in Acts 3, signs and wonders in Acts 2 and 5, Peter and Dorcas in Acts 9, and Paul and Eutychus in Acts 20. In the epistles, Paul mentions "gifts of healings" in 1 Corinthians 12:28. He also mentions that he left Trophimus sick at Miletus (2 Timothy 4:20), and he told Timothy to take some wine for his stomach's sake (1 Timothy 5:23). Healing receives relatively little mention because the emphasis is on the spread of the gospel across the Roman Empire.

A brief survey of 2000 years of church history reveals that from the very beginning, Christians have believed in ministering to the sick and the dying. No dichotomy ever existed between medicine and prayer. Christians have led the way in starting hospitals, clinics, sanitariums, rest homes, and hospice care. In the Chicago area, for example, we have Rush Presbyterian-St. Luke's Hospital, Christ Hospital, Lutheran General Hospital, Good Samaritan Hospital, Resurrection Hospital, to name just a few. Christians have always believed that part of their message involves offering help for the sick and dying in the name of Jesus Christ.

I should also mention that recent medical research backs up the relationship between medicine and prayer. In the last few years a whole host of studies has validated the fact that when people of faith pray for the sick, the sick get better. This isn't speculation; it's a fact that has been confirmed over and over again by rigorous scientific studies (see "Science

Finds God" in *Prayer, Faith and Healing* [Rodale Press, 1999], pp. 3-17).

And in recent years there has been a renewed emphasis on the importance of praying for the sick. In some churches this has become a major ministry involving healing services and teams of laypeople trained to pray for and minister to the sick. It's also fair to say that in some circles there has been ambivalence on this subject. I think some people are frightened of the perceived excesses of others (I'm thinking of certain flamboyant practices of the "healing evangelists" on late-night Christian television). Perhaps we are embarrassed by the possibility of failure. Certainly we don't want to raise false hopes. And we definitely don't want to lose our focus on the gospel as our central message.

All these concerns are quite valid. And yet if you ask around, it's evident that God can and sometimes does work miracles in answer to prayer. And we all have a story to tell in this regard. My story goes back to the church I pastored in Garland, Texas. One day a woman named Libby Redwine asked if the elders would anoint her with oil and pray over her in accordance with James 5. No one had ever asked me to do that before, and I didn't know what to say. The elders didn't have any experience in this area either, but they agreed we should do it. So I went to the grocery store and bought a jar of olive oil. It just seemed like the right thing to do. The next Sunday after the worship service, Libby and the elders gathered in my office. I was there along with John Grassmick, Bob Peabody, Nate Schnitman, and David Hebert. I read James 5:13-16 and asked Libby to tell us what we should pray for. Libby said that years earlier she had had one of the first open-heart surgeries in Texas. Evidently her arteries were in terrible shape because the doctor said they were like chalk and would snap if he tried to operate again. Tests showed that Libby had developed a life-threatening blockage in her lower abdomen. Surgery was scheduled for the following Tuesday.

After asking Libby if she had any sins she wished to confess, I dipped my finger in the oil and made the sign of the cross on her forehead. The elders laid their hands on her, and one by one, we prayed earnestly that God might heal her. As we began to pray, "something" happened that I can't fully explain. All of us were aware of the powerful presence of God in the room. When we finished, Libby had a big smile on her face and we all knew that God had met with us as we prayed. The next day Libby had presurgery tests. On Tuesday she called with an amazing report. The surgery had been canceled because the tests revealed that the blockage had disappeared. She was giddy with excitement when she told me the good news. The surgery was never performed. And from that day on, she and I and the elders believed that God had healed her in answer to our prayers.

When I told that story in a sermon last year, Dr. Mark Bailey, president of Dallas Seminary, asked me if I had other stories like that. A few, I replied, but not many, and nothing as dramatic as that. Looking back over the years, I can tell of numerous occasions when I have prayed for someone and they have gotten better. Yet there have also been times when prayers have been offered and no improvement could be detected. Dr. Bailey and I agreed that this is the experience of most pastors. From time to time, it seems as if God is pleased to grant an amazing deliverance, sometimes a complete healing, that appears to come solely through prayer. Why doesn't that happen all the time? To answer that question more fully would take another chapter, or more probably, another book, and in the end, we still can't be certain as to the answer. But what we do know is that God has given us clear instructions about praying for the sick. With that in mind, let's take a closer look at what James 5:14-15 says.

A Four-Step Process

If we look at James 5:14-15 carefully, we discover that it mentions four steps in the process of praying for the sick.

Step 1: The Sick Person Calls for the Elders

"Is any one of you sick? He should call the elders of the church to pray over him" (James 5:14). The process begins when the sick person calls for the elders to come to him. The word "sick" is very broad. It includes any serious physical, mental, emotional, spiritual, or relational problem that has become too heavy to bear. There are many kinds of sickness, and when a believer is overwhelmed by such, he should feel free to call the elders to come to him.

Who are the "elders" of the church? Certainly, the term refers to the elected spiritual leaders of the congregation. Taken in its broadest sense, the term refers to any group of godly Christians who have a concern for the sick. But why are the elders to come to the sick person? No doubt the sick person is unable to come to the church, so the church comes to him. And he may be too sick to pray for himself, so the church comes to pray for him. A friend reminded me of the book written by Joseph Cardinal Bernardin during his struggle with cancer—a struggle that finally took his life. Cardinal Bernardin placed great stress on the importance of praying for the sick because they are too weak to pray for themselves. Sometimes the sick person will be mentally unable to sustain coherent thoughts. Chemotherapy or other drugs may have sapped all mental and physical energy and left him somewhat disoriented. The pain may be so great that prayer becomes a burden. The patient may be in a coma or may drift in and out of consciousness. Those who are healthy can perform a great service for the sick by praying for them. This is an example of the strong bearing the burdens of the weak.

Finally, why call the elders? First, because the elders represent the church. Instead of having the whole church come, the church can be represented by the elders. Second, the elders are preeminently to be men of prayer. They are called to do this because true elders know how to get in touch with God.

Step 2: The Elders Go to the Sick Person

This step follows from the first. The elders go wherever the sick person is. They go together because there is strength in numbers. Praying in person makes their prayers much more fervent, heartfelt, and earnest. And their presence encourages the sick person with the message that "the church has not forgotten you." And since elders lead by example, they show the whole congregation how to care for the sick in their midst.

As I read James 5:14, I picture a scene where the person is too sick to sit up in bed, so the elders gather around the bed, lift up holy hands, and literally pray over the sick person.

Step 3: The Elders Pray and Anoint with Oil

"He should call the elders of the church to pray over him and anoint him with oil in the name of the Lord" (James 5:14). Prayer is the key. When the elders come to pray for the sick person, as part of their visit, they are to anoint him with oil. The word literally means to "rub" oil on him, almost like a massage. The kind of oil used here is not identified, but we can be sure it does not refer to motor oil. Most likely the reference is to olive oil, since that was widely used in the first century. But the precise kind of oil doesn't matter. Some missionary friends asked their church in Nigeria to send the elders to pray over their son who was very sick and seemed to be getting worse. The elders and the pastor came to the home and asked the missionaries for some oil. The only oil they had was peanut oil, so that is what the elders used. That very day, the young boy began to get better.

In the Bible, oil was often used as a symbol of health and vitality from the Lord. Kings were anointed with oil as a visible symbol of God's presence and the need for His blessing. The same is true in James 5. The oil isn't magical. There is no supernatural power in a few drops (or a few cups, for that matter) of oil—olive, peanut, or any other kind. The oil is a simple aid to faith. It is a humbling reminder that all healing must come from God. In this sense, the oil is like the bread and wine of the Lord's Supper. It builds faith and says to the sick person, "God is here and He is able to heal you." Sometimes I have done this sort of praying in a hospital room where the sick person is wired up to all sorts of high-tech monitors. The simple act of anointing with oil serves to remind all of us—the sick person and the ones doing the praying—that it is the Lord who heals and that our trust is not in technology (as good as it is) but in God alone.

Note that the anointing is to be done "in the name of the Lord." This is all-important because it reminds us that God is the ultimate source of all blessing and all healing.

There is no power in the elders.

There is no power in the oil.

But there is enormous power, omnipotent power, eternal power, in the name of the Lord. He alone can grant the needed healing.

Step 4: There Is Healing and Forgiveness

The fourth step is described in James 5:15: "The prayer offered in faith will make the sick person well; the Lord will raise him up. If he has sinned, he will be forgiven." This step is simply the expected result of steps 1–3: The sick person is healed and his sins are forgiven. James uses an unusual phrase to describe the prayer. He calls it "the prayer offered in faith." This particular phrase is used nowhere else in the New Testament. In one sense, every sincere prayer must be offered in faith or it can hardly be called prayer at all. When the elders pray, they are to come to God with an attitude of complete trust that He can and will do what is needed in every situation. But it is also possible that the "prayer of faith" means something like the gift of faith mentioned in 1 Corinthians 12:9. Since faith itself is a gift from God (and not something worked up by our own enthusiasm), perhaps James means to say that when God wants to heal someone, He gives the elders the faith to pray that way with great confidence. Looking back on my experience in which the elders and I prayed for Libby Redwine, we truly did sense the presence of God in a remarkable way.

The text says nothing about how the healing will come. It doesn't demand a miraculous or instantaneous healing. Nor does the healing in view rule out the use of medical care. Whether quickly or slowly, by miracle or by medicine, or by some combination of the two, God is able to heal His children.

And it is certainly important to note the close relationship between the physical and the spiritual. The Greek construction of the "if" clause suggests that sin may indeed be involved in the sickness. Not all sickness is caused by a particular sin, but some illnesses stem directly from our sinful actions and attitudes. Until those things are confronted and confessed, it is pointless to pray for healing. Whenever I am asked to anoint the sick with oil, I always inquire as to their spiritual condition and I ask if they are conscious of any sin that is standing between them and God, blocking His healing power. Sometimes they make a confession, sometimes they don't. But it is important to ask the question in every case. And in rare situations I may refuse to pray for healing or to anoint with oil if I sense the sick person has a hardened heart or a rebellious spirit. In that case, to pray for healing might actually oppose God's work of divine chastisement that is intended to bring the sick person to a place of personal repentance.

Notice that James 5:15 says the prayer offered in faith "will make the sick person well; the Lord will raise him up." For many of us, that seems too confident and too dogmatic. James states without any qualification that the sick person will be healed. Period. No ifs, ands, or buts about it. We would prefer the verse to say that "the prayer of faith *may* save the sick." After all, most of us have prayed for people who got worse instead of better. I recall that Len Hoppe (a godly man and a former elder of the church I pastor) fervently believed that God was going to heal him of cancer as a testimony to the world of God's power. Up until the very day of surgery, he proclaimed his belief to everyone he met. And multitudes of people at Calvary Memorial Church poured their hearts out to God on Len's behalf. Two weeks after the surgery, I officiated at his funeral service.

A Proper Perspective

It is an undeniable fact that not everyone we pray for and not everyone we anoint is healed. There are various ways of dealing with this reality, and none of them satisfy me completely. There is a mystery here that I cannot fully explain. I do think it helps to compare this passage with other statements about prayer in the New Testament where similar sweeping promises are made. Those statements are meant to encourage us about the boundless possibilities of prayer. They encourage us to believe that no situation is hopeless for God. Just because the doctors have given up doesn't mean the Great Physician has given up.

How, then, should we pray for the sick? Three words come to mind. We should pray...

- *Aggressively* because nothing is impossible with God.

- *Fervently* because the fervent prayers of the righteous are powerful (James 5:16).

- *Submissively* because God's understanding of the total situation is much greater than ours. Just because we think physical healing would be best doesn't mean God agrees with us. We should ask for what we want without telling God how to answer our prayers.

During my research for this chapter I came across a statement regarding healing that has been bouncing around in my mind ever since I read it. Most of us think of healing as "getting rid of the disease." It's like running the clock of life backwards and restoring the person to their previous state. *But in the Bible, healing is a very broad concept that involves coming into a right relationship with God first and foremost.* Then it touches every part of life—body, soul, and spirit. It involves the healing of all broken relationships and brings us to a place where we can receive God's blessings in a new and powerful way. That alone is a huge concept that goes far beyond "Pray for my son, who broke his arm in football practice." Here's the quote that started me thinking in a new direction: "Healing in the Bible is not becoming what we were but becoming all that God intends us to be." Think about that for a while. When we pray for healing, we dare not focus on the physical to the exclusion of the spiritual, emotional, and relational facets of life. We are not healed until we are made whole on every level of our existence.

Our Response to James 5:14-15

Becoming People of Prayer

As I survey James 5:14-15 in light of the whole Bible, the following two statements seem absolutely true to me:

- It is not always God's will to heal physically, or no sick believer would ever die.

- It is often God's will to heal; otherwise James 5:14-15 would not be in the Bible.

Sometimes we focus on one statement to the exclusion of the other, but both seem entirely true to me. Part of our problem is that we have lost our faith in 1) God's will to heal, and 2) the role of the elders in the healing process.

I believe God has made four provisions for sick believers:

- The caring community of faith—the church

- Loving family and friends

- Doctors, nurses, hospitals, and medicine

- Godly elders who pray for the sick

We have robbed the sick of that last provision. But it is still in the Bible. Sometimes we overlook the basic need of prayer. We send cards, flowers, and candy. We offer baby-sitting and we prepare meals for the sick. We are ready to run errands. This is all good and proper and a wonderful expression of our faith. But let us not forget that the sick need our prayers more than they need anything else. In our haste to help them, we must start with prayer and let everything else be added to it. We can say it this way:

All believers ought to pray for the sick.

> *Praying for the sick is the special duty and privilege of the elders of the church.*

This tells us what kind of men the elders should be: *godly men of prayer.* If they are not men of prayer away from the bedside, they will do little to help the sick and dying. In order for their prayers to make a difference, they must be men of vital, living faith, ready to pray even in desperate circumstances.

Trusting God's Response to Our Prayers

Based on James 5:14-15, praying for the sick should be the normal work of the church. This is a noble ministry that should be recovered in our day. Perhaps we would see God's power manifest in greater ways if we dared to believe and obey His Word.

At the same time, we must let God be God. He knows what is best, and there are certain principles we need to keep in mind as we pray:

1. *Only God is sovereign, and we cannot know in advance what the outcome of our prayers will be.* Therefore, we should pray with humility, not making promises we can't keep. At the end of the day, God is God and we are not. We must keep this perspective before us while we pray for the sick.

2. *Since God is omnipotent, we should expect that God will move from heaven in answer to our prayers, yet often in ways we cannot humanly explain.* Therefore, we should pray boldly and ask God for the healing we seek. Sometimes while visiting the sick, we may feel almost intimidated by the gravity of the situation. But if we have our eyes upon God, we will not fear to ask Him to heal His children.

3. *Since everything God creates is good, we should view both prayer and medicine as gifts to help us when we are sick.* This point seems obvious to me, but it may be controversial to some people. God doesn't ask us to choose between prayer and medicine. Pray, and take your pills to the glory of God. Seek the Lord when you are weak and ask for His help. And do not despise His help if it comes in the form of surgery or chemotherapy.

4. *Since God knows what is best, we must believe that when healing does not come, it is for our good and His glory.* This is nothing more than a summary of what Romans 8:28 teaches. Sometimes we will see this very clearly and others times we must choose to believe it by faith. But it is still true in every case whether we fully understand it or not.

5. *Since faith is a gift from God, we understand that God will give the faith to believe when He wants to move in unusual power.* In any case, our job is always to pray regardless of our own "feelings" one way or the other. Many times when I pray for the sick I am not certain how God intends to answer my prayers. But as I am fond of saying, when it comes to God's work, I'm in sales, not administration, and I'm not responsible for the answers, only for the praying. I do believe that sometimes as we pray, we will sense God's presence in an unusual way. If someone is healed in answer to our prayers, it is not our faith that did the healing. Faith is only an instrument for God's power, and even faith itself is a gift from God.

6. *Since sin may block God's healing power, we are fully justified to inquire as to a person's spiritual state before we pray for them.* I would even say we should

not pray for healing when we are aware that the sick person has unconfessed sin or has shown persistent disobedience or wrong attitudes. I am not suggesting that we turn a prayer for healing into a confession of every possible sin. But I believe that compassionate elders will know how to deal wisely with the sheep who are entrusted to their care. Certainly we need to ask, "Are you aware of anything in your life that may have brought this sickness upon you or is hindering God's healing power?" When the answer is yes, we can then deal with that issue as part of the whole healing process.

7. *Since God's Word is true, we glorify Him when we obey His Word, regardless of the outcome.* This is a point author John Armstrong brings home strongly in his article "Is Any Among You Sick?" (*Viewpoint*, May-June 2000). In December 1999 I joined a number of Chicago-area pastors in praying that God would heal John of a severe case of Chronic Fatigue Syndrome. In his article based on that time of prayer, he notes that the pastors agreed that we didn't fully understand James 5:14-15 and that we also agreed we didn't have to understand it all to obey the part we did understand. "After all, worship and obedience always engage us in mystery, the mystery of who God is and what God reveals." God doesn't call us to understand every detail in advance. We are to obey what we do know and then leave the results with Him.

Key Truths About Healing

Earthly Healings Are Partial and Temporary

There is one final word that needs to be said before we move on. *As important as healing is, we must remember that all healing in this life is partial and temporary.* Ultimate healing will not come until the dead in Christ are raised when Jesus comes again (1 Thessalonians 4:13-18). This strikes me as a very important point. Sometimes we speak of believers who died after a long illness as having been healed in heaven. But the Bible doesn't say it that way. It's true that those who die in Christ are with Him in heaven from the moment of their earthly death. And it's also true that their sufferings in every sense are over forever. But as long as their physical bodies lie buried in the ground, we should not say that they have been truly healed. We won't be completely healed until our mortal bodies put on immortality in the resurrection when Christ returns. Biblical salvation includes the redemption of the body, not just the redemption of the soul in heaven. If we deny or downplay the physical resurrection of believers, we are no better off than the followers of various Eastern religions who don't believe in any sort of resurrection of the body.

As I write these words I'm thinking of my dear friend Gary Olson, who died in 1999. I know that he is in heaven and I know that his suffering is over, and I also know he is in a state of perfect heavenly joy. Is he in a better place? Yes. Has he been healed? Not completely. Not as long as his mortal remains are still on the earth. I will not be satisfied until I see him once again, hear his hearty laugh, and feel him put his arm on my shoulder and say with his distinctive deep voice, "Pastor Ray, how are you doing?" Dreams and visions are fine, and memories are sweet, but nothing can take the place of seeing our loved ones once again.

Earthly Healings Are a Foretaste of Things to Come

If I think of it that way, then the question of physical healing comes into proper focus. Can God heal the sick? Yes. Does He? All the time. Does God sometimes move from heaven to deliver someone from desperate illness? Yes, and

I think it happens more often than we expect. *We should rejoice in every healing, no matter how large or small it seems to us.* But let's remember that everyone healed in this life will die eventually. Death still reigns on planet earth. It's almost as if God is saying, "So you're impressed with what I can do about cancer? Just wait till you see what I can do with a dead person." All physical healing is like a tiny down payment, a deposit, a tantalizing foretaste, a guarantee of greater miracles to come when the dead in Christ are raised and transformed at the Second Coming. When I think of all the people whose funerals I officiated at over the years and how much I miss them, I want to say, "Lord Jesus, come back today. Empty the graveyards, and let the celebration begin!"

Of the 41 people who experienced the miracle of healing in the Gospels, all died eventually. And my friend Libby Redwine died several years ago. She lived 12 or 13 years after we prayed for her (for which I give thanks to God), but even she went the way of all flesh. As I will, too, unless I should live until the rapture of the saints.

Our Part, God's Part

Why are some prayers for healing answered and some not? There is no one answer that can fully explain God's purposes, but I am content with the words of Psalm 115:3: "Our God is in heaven; he does whatever pleases him." I can state my own theology of prayer for healing in one sentence: *We do the praying, and God does the healing—in His own time, in His own way, according to His own will.* We are to pray earnestly, fervently, unitedly, repeatedly, obediently, and with all the faith God gives us. We are to do our part, and God will not fail to do His.

I come to the end of this chapter with great joy in my heart even as I bow before the mystery of a God whose ways are far beyond my meager understanding. Through prayer we have the privilege of lifting the burden from our brothers and sisters. Through prayer we may become agents of healing to those who are sick. What an honor to be used of God in this way!

Here is my final exhortation: Let us pray boldly, confidently, humbly, and in faith, believing that as we pray for the sick and dying, God hears, He cares, and He will do what is best in every situation. When we pray for the sick, we are doing the work of Jesus in the world. Fear not, keep believing, and keep on praying.

CHAPTER 6

His Faithfulness
to the Fearful

Some prayers are harder to pray than others. I learned that many years ago when my father died. One October day he felt a pain in his shoulder. The doctors later said it was transferred pain from a bacterial infection elsewhere in his body. It did not seem serious at first, but he got no better and a few days later traveled by ambulance to Birmingham, where a battery of doctors went to work on him. Marlene and I drove in from Dallas, arriving at the hospital sometime after midnight. Dad spoke to me when I saw him, and I could tell he was desperately ill.

A few days later, back in Dallas, we received the dreaded call. Once again we flew through the night to Birmingham, hoping against hope. But my untrained eyes told me that he was not long for this world. That day—it is etched forever in my mind—I went in to see him and he did not know me. He was drugged and nearly in a coma. Leaning against the wall outside the Intensive Care Unit I wept furious tears, unable to keep back the truth—my dad was dying and I could do nothing about it.

I must have prayed that day. I'm sure I did. After all, I was in seminary learning to help other people draw near to God. But if I prayed, I do not remember it. In that terrible moment of utter helplessness, prayer did not come naturally.

All theology aside, I knew my father was dying. So I could hardly pray, "O God, heal him," for I knew in my soul that God was not going to answer that prayer. But I could not pray, "O God, take him home and end the pain," for he was my father and much too young to die. So I prayed something. Exactly what, I do not remember. In a few days, God mercifully intervened and ended my father's ordeal.

Years passed, I finished seminary, and Marlene and I moved to Downey, California, where I settled into my first pastorate. After several years of trying, we were delighted when Marlene finally became pregnant. The pregnancy was not especially difficult and we looked forward to the day when our first child would be born. We had to wait longer, almost ten months, but at last labor pains signaled that the blessed event was only a few hours away. After a long, hard night of labor, there were some problems. The doctor came in about 5:15 A.M. and said, "We're going to take that baby now." It wasn't a question, it was a statement of fact. As they rolled my wife away, I saw the fear on her face and felt so helpless. When she disappeared behind the door of the operating room, I bowed my head and tried to pray, but no words would come out. That had never happened before. Always I could find words to frame my thoughts. But suddenly I could not pray. It was a combination of fatigue from the long hours at the hospital, shock from the doctor's announcement, the look on my wife's face, and the unspoken fear that something might happen to the baby or to her. Sitting alone in that confused, exhausted, frightened state, I bowed my head and tried to pray. No words came out. Nothing. No thoughts even came to my mind. I could not think of any Bible verses. All I could do was to stammer out, "O God...O God...O God...Lord Jesus, have mercy."

A few minutes later (though it seemed like an hour) a nurse said, "You can come in now." There was my wife, in pain but still conscious, and there on the table was a brand-new baby boy. I knew that God had answered my prayers even though I couldn't put the words together. Looking back on that experience, I learned something profound. *The more something means to you, the harder it is to pray for it.* The reason we can pray so easily for others is that we're not that deeply invested in them. It's relatively easy to say a brief prayer for people in Thailand or Botswana or Latvia. After all, you don't know them personally and you'll probably never meet them and you don't have any personal investment in them. It is much different when you try to pray for those who are closest to you. The more you care, the harder it is to pray. When it comes to those things in life that really matter to you—your husband, your wife, your children, your loved ones—they are hard to pray for because they are close to your heart.

Romans 8:26-27 assures us that when we can't pray, the Holy Spirit prays for us. When we can't find the words, the Holy Spirit speaks to the Father with groans that can't be put in words. And when we aren't sure how to pray, the Holy Spirit prays for us according to the will of God. This is a wonderful provision from God because as we go through life, we face many situations where we simply don't know how to pray. In those moments, we can be sure that God the Holy Spirit is praying for us.

Our Weakness

Romans 8:26 begins, "In the same way, the Spirit helps us in our weakness. We do not know what we ought to pray for." The word "helps" is a rich word that pictures someone helping another carry a heavy load. Imagine someone trying to drag an enormous log but it's so heavy he can barely move it. Then along comes a strong man who picks up one end and together they carry the log down the road. That's what the Holy Spirit does. He continually comes to us and helps us with our heavy load.

We need the Spirit's help because we are so weak. The word "weakness" is the same word used for sickness in James 5:14. It refers to those moments in life when we are physically, mentally, emotionally, and spiritually exhausted. Circumstances have combined to push us over the edge. But it refers to more than momentary difficulty. *Weakness is our condition on the earth.* We are inherently weak and unable to help ourselves. Some of us realize this truth, while the rest of us try to muddle through on our own. Here is the proof: *We don't know how to pray as we ought.* Literally, this means we don't know what to pray for. And this is one of our chief problems in prayer. How many times have we tried to pray and we didn't know what to ask from the Lord? This happens often when we are faced with a crisis or when we try to pray for someone else. In the first place, we don't know the future, so we can't tell how things will turn out. Second, we don't know what is best for us. We may think we want a new job because we can't stand our boss, but if we were to get a new job, we could also end up with a boss who is ten times worse. On a deeper level, married people may dream of being single again (or single people may wish they were married), but when you are, you discover that you exchanged one set of problems for another.

And so it goes. *We don't know what to pray for because our vision is so limited.* We see only a tiny fraction of the universe, and our perspective is inevitably tainted by selfishness. How can we be sure that what we are praying for is what God wants? Ecclesiastes 6:12 says this very poignantly: "Who knows what is good for a man in life, during the few and meaningless days he passes through like a shadow?" The answer is, we don't know what is good for us. When we were little our mothers said, "Eat your broccoli; it's good for you." But we're not so sure anymore. In fact, we're not so sure about anything.

For over 30 years Dr. James Montgomery Boice served as pastor of Tenth Presbyterian Church in Philadelphia. This church was made famous during the ministry of Dr. Donald Grey Barnhouse. For generations it has been a Bible-teaching center in the heart of Philadelphia. Shortly after Boice was diagnosed with liver cancer, he made a brief announcement to his congregation about his illness and the course of treatment he was pursuing. In his comments he addressed the question regarding how people should pray for him. "Should we pray for a miracle?" he asked. Not necessarily. There is no doubt, he said, that God can work miracles. *But the God who works miracles could have prevented the cancer in the first place.* He asked prayer for the doctors, that they might have wisdom in pursuing the proper course of treatment. Then he spoke of the goodness of God and said that even his cancer was for his own good in the long run. He also recognized that humanly speaking, his life might well be measured in weeks, not months or years. He died several months later.

I was comforted and humbled as I read Dr. Boice's words. His faith shines through and shows itself in the very weakness Paul is talking about in Romans 8:26. Dr. Boice did not know what God wanted to do through this sudden attack of liver cancer. Perhaps God would heal him. As it turned out, Dr. Boice was soon home in heaven. He pointed out that the one thing he could be certain of was that God is good even in the midst of what turned out to be terminal cancer. He was not certain of anything else regarding his illness.

So it is for all of us most of the time. Rarely can we be absolutely sure what God wants to do in a particular situation. After we have made our requests to God, especially regarding the crisis issues of life, we must cry out, "But

Father, I don't know what You want. And I want Your will to be done—even if it means my will is not done in this situation. I truly believe that You know best."

A friend at a local high school gave me a tape of a speech Gary Olson made in April 1998. Gary was a former elder of our church and for many years was the head football coach at Oak Park-River Forest High School. He made the speech eight months after his heart surgery in 1997 and a year and a half before his sudden death in November 1999. On the tape, Gary gives a short talk to a group of Christian coaches on the subject of handling the hard times of life. He began by mentioning his lung cancer in the early 1980s, which led to his coming to Christ. Then in 1989 his wife, Dawn, was in a terrible accident that nearly took her life. Gary stepped down from coaching for a while so he could help her. The hardest blows came in 1997. In August of that year he collapsed during football practice and was taken to a hospital, where the doctors discovered he had an enlarged heart. A few days later he had surgery to replace a defective heart valve. At about the same time he faced a crisis in his family. A month or so later, his mother suddenly died of a brain hemorrhage. It seemed almost too much to bear. On the tape he said that he had called his pastor and asked, "How should I pray?" His pastor told him to pray, "Lord, have mercy. God, have mercy. Jesus, have mercy."

I was his pastor, and also a very good friend. I smiled when I heard him tell the story because I had forgotten that phone call. Then it all came back to me. My answer was off the top of my head, but in retrospect I believe it was perfectly biblical. There are many times in life when the only thing we can do is to cry out, "God, have mercy. Lord, have mercy. Jesus, have mercy."

The Spirit's Help

He Intercedes for Us

Romans 8:26 continues, "The Spirit himself intercedes for us with groans that words cannot express." We need the help of the Holy Spirit because we don't know how to pray. Paul says the Spirit intercedes for us with groans that cannot be expressed in words. (Literally, "wordless groanings.") *In those moments when we cannot pray, the Holy Spirit prays for us.* When we lift up our feeble and even ignorant prayers to God, the Holy Spirit takes them and translates them into the language of heaven.

No one knows exactly how this happens because it is a ministry that goes on between the Spirit and the Father. But I imagine it could happen like this: We may pray for a new job, but the Holy Spirit intercedes and says: "Father, he thinks he wants a new job because he is weary of the pressure. But I know it is Your will that he learn to depend entirely on You. So Father, please don't give him the new job right now. Give him supernatural strength and please send along a Christian who can give him some encouragement." And because the Holy Spirit always prays according to the will of God, that's the prayer that is answered.

Bible commentator Matthew Henry says the Holy Spirit "excites praying graces." He makes us want to pray, He teaches us how to pray, and He helps us as we pray. And when we can't pray at all, He prays for us to the Father. What a blessed promise and encouragement this is! Sometimes we are so confused, so worried, so hurried, so harried, so pressured, so ill, so distracted, so tired, and so weary that words will not come. But often, the best prayers are unheard and even unspoken. They arise from a broken heart to God, who hears the groanings that cannot be put in words.

He Prays According to God's Will

How do we know that God hears those inarticulate groanings that come from deep within? Romans 8:27 declares that God constantly searches our hearts: "He who searches our hearts knows the mind of the Spirit, because the Spirit intercedes for the saints in accordance with God's will." Because the Father knows what the Spirit is thinking, there is perfect intimacy and perfect harmony. There is no contradiction between the Holy Spirit who indwells us and the Father in heaven. When the Spirit intercedes for us, He always intercedes according to God's will. So when we pray, and say what is on our hearts, the Spirit says to the Father, "What he really means is this.... If he knew better, this is what he would ask for.... She wants to be like Jesus, and this is what she really needs."

God already knows our deepest desires. Sometimes we talk about having an "unspoken prayer request." In the old days, during a prayer meeting the leader would ask, "How many have an unspoken prayer request?" Almost every hand would go up. Unspoken prayer requests are so close to our heart that we dare not mention them in public. They are deep and precious and private. Sometimes we could not mention them without tears. Romans 8:27 reminds us that there are no "unspoken requests" with God. There's an old gospel song that says, "Jesus knows our every weakness." And He does. He knows what we need before we ask Him.

An Ever-Present Ministry

There is great encouragement in Romans 8:26-27 even though we may not see it at first. Our suffering, our uncertainty, our struggle with prayer, our doubt and confusion, and our worry over the future reveal our weakness. It strips away the mask of self-sufficiency and displays our utter helplessness. It forces us to confront our own inabilities. We are forced to

say, "I'm not as strong as I thought I was. I'm not invincible."
And the Holy Spirit comes alongside to help us in our need.
The Spirit, who is the third member of the Trinity, prays to
the Father (the first member of the Trinity) in the name of the
Son (the second member of the Trinity) for us in our
moment of weakness. It is God praying to God in God's
name on behalf of God's children! What an amazing thought
this is. In your weakness, when you feel desperate about
the things that truly matter to you and you don't know what
to say, and all you can do is cry out, "Oh God!" the message
is, "Don't worry. That's enough because there is Someone
who is praying for you."

We know that Jesus is in heaven praying for us (see
Romans 8:34). But there's more: When you come to the
moment of complete exhaustion and can no longer frame
the words, you don't have to worry. The Holy Spirit will
pray for you. In your weakness, He is strong. When you
cannot speak, He speaks for you. When we lean against the
wall of desperation, crying out to God—when we whisper,
"God, I don't know what to say. I don't know how to pray
about this"—the Holy Spirit comes alongside and says,
"Don't worry. I'll pray for you." And He does.

As I studied Romans 8:26-27, I got some help from dear
old Martin Luther. Writing almost 500 years ago, he commented that it's a good thing if we occasionally receive the
opposite of what we pray for because that's a sign the Holy
Spirit is at work in our life. We may be praying, "Lord, do this
and this and this." Meanwhile, the Holy Spirit is saying,
"Lord, what he means is this. Don't pay any attention to that.
He said thus-and-so. If he saw the bigger picture, he'd really
ask for such-and-such." As we pray from our weak and limited perspective, the Holy Spirit "corrects" our prayers, so to
speak, so that God's will is always done even in our most
wrong-headed prayers. Because the Holy Spirit knows what
God's will is, and because God searches our hearts, He is

able to pray for us in ways that always correspond with God's will. One sign that this is happening is that we pray for one thing and God does the opposite.

Does that mean our prayers are in vain? Not at all. Does it mean we shouldn't pray? Not at all. It simply reveals our inherent human weakness and the limitation of our perspective on life. We see the part, the Holy Spirit sees the whole. We see one little piece, the Holy Spirit sees the big picture. We pray according to the little bit that we see, the Holy Spirit prays according to His perfect knowledge.

Our Response

What should this truth do for our faith?

1. *It should encourage us to pray with great confidence.* God is not judging your words, but listening to your heart. We pray to a God who can discern the prayer within the prayer. He hears the words we say and He also understands the heart cry and the hidden desires that lie underneath our prayers. He can give us the substance of what we ask for even while refusing the form they take. That is, He can say yes to our deepest desires even while He says no on the surface. Thus, we get what we truly desired even though it is not what we asked for.

2. *It should teach us that our salvation rests in God alone.* Romans 8 teaches us that the entire Trinity is involved in our salvation. We know that God hears our prayers, and this chapter tells us that Jesus is in heaven interceding for us and the Holy Spirit is on earth interceding for us. What could be better than that? We've got the Father in heaven, Jesus at His right hand, and the Holy Spirit within. This is why we have eternal security. For a believer to end up in hell,

the Holy Spirit would have to fail in His intercession. You may be weak, but the Holy Spirit is praying for you right now.

We have a Trinitarian salvation:

God called you.

Jesus saved you.

The Holy Spirit intercedes for you.

How can you ever be lost? *Your salvation rests upon the work of the Trinity.* The Father, Son, and Holy Spirit would all have to fail before you could ever be eternally lost. Better that the sun refuse to shine than for our Triune God to fail. Better that the planets should reverse their rotation and time go backward than for God to fail. It cannot happen; it will not happen. All of God's sheep will show up in heaven. Not one will be lost. He knows them; He calls them all by name; and every single one will be safe in the sheepfold in the end.

Our Assurance

Romans 8:26-27 tells us that when we are so discouraged, when the pain is too deep, when the disappointment too profound, when the sense of loss so overwhelming that we can't put it into words, the Holy Spirit says, "My child, I understand. Let me take over. I'll talk to God for you." And He prays for us with groans that words cannot express. Even when no one else cares or knows or understands, even when we can't understand anything around us, even when the present is bleak and the future a dark mystery, the Son in heaven and the Holy Spirit on earth are interceding for us. We are being prayed for by the #1 Prayer Team in the universe. One member is above, one member is below, and we're right in the middle. That ought to encourage us.

God has given us the gift of prayer. It was never meant to be a burden, but rather, a source of unlimited blessing for us and for those around us. And God has made it possible for us to pray about anything, anytime, anywhere. When we can't pray, when the words won't come, when we don't know what to pray for, we have the Spirit within us, who prays for us. What an honor, what a privilege, what a gift. And what a God, who would make such provision for us!

CHAPTER 7

His Faithfulness
to the Fallen

I recently received an e-mail message from my college roommate—a man I haven't seen since 1974. He wrote to ask if I had heard the news. What news? Another friend from our college days had divorced his wife and was now pursuing the former wife of a classmate from those same college days. Two friends, two marriages broken, one man now pursuing his former friend's former wife. Did I mention that the man who is doing the pursuing is a pastor?

Then just a few days ago I received another e-mail message—this time from a friend I met in seminary. I haven't seen him since 1978. He wrote me a nice note that included these two sentences:

> In this world of ours it is never a sure thing, never to be assumed that someone we knew in seminary is continuing in the faith. I have heard too many horror stories of broken marriages and wrecked ministries.

Those two messages set me to thinking. I was struck by the fact that I received them so close in time from friends who don't know each other and whom I haven't seen in decades. Yet their messages were nearly identical.

I do not bring up those examples simply to bemoan the fact that spiritual leaders fall into grievous sin. That much is evident from a simple reading of the Bible. There is Noah, who got drunk; Abraham, who lied about his wife; Moses, who murdered an Egyptian; and of course, there is David, who committed adultery and then had a man murdered to cover up his sin.

But for the Grace of God

The question I am asking is this: Why does God allow such things to happen? Why does He allow good men to fall into sin—and what are we to learn from this? I'm sure we all know one answer already: *God allows good people to fall into sin so that the rest of us will learn not to make the same mistake.* That's true, of course. How many of us have heard bad news about a friend and said, "There but for the grace of God go I?" I have said that to myself many times—and so have you. It's perfectly true that we can all take a lesson from the mistakes of others—and if we don't, we may find ourselves wishing we had.

But there is much more to be learned, and that is the burden of this chapter. I want us to take a closer look at Peter, who three times denied his Lord. Perhaps the place to begin is with a simple reading of the story. Ponder these words Jesus spoke to Peter on the night before He was crucified. "Simon, Simon, Satan has asked to sift you as wheat. But I have prayed for you, Simon, that your faith may not fail. And when you have turned back, strengthen your brothers" (Luke 22:31-32). These words must have seemed strange to Peter, coming as it were out of the blue. It has been well remarked that Peter in many ways was the most human of all the disciples. He constantly got into trouble because he blurted out the stuff everyone else was thinking but didn't have the guts to say. He was the man with the foot-shaped mouth, constantly promising more than he could deliver.

This night is no exception. When he hears these words of Jesus, he knows without being told that they contain a great rebuke—a prediction of personal failure that must have seemed impossible. But Peter is nothing if not brave at heart, so he replies foolishly but honestly, "Lord, I am ready to go with you to prison and to death" (Luke 22:33). He did not know that years later he would keep that promise. But not that night. As he uttered those words, his moment of greatest personal failure—the blot that 2000 years cannot remove from his record—his threefold denial of Christ was less than five hours away.

Ponder the words of Jesus for a moment: "But when you have turned back." The King James Version says it this way: "But when you are converted." Some people have stumbled over that statement, but I think it is entirely accurate. The words of our Lord hang in the air with a message we need to hear. It is entirely possible to be an "unconverted" Christian. Peter was saved, but in some deep sense, he was not yet fully converted to the Master's use—and that explains his tragic failure.

This is a message from God we all need to hear. For just a moment, let me speak directly to the men who are reading this book. Deep down inside, most of us want to walk with God and we want our lives to count for Him. We want to be good husbands and fathers, and we want to set a good example for our children. We truly want to be the salt of the earth and the light of the world. That's our desire, our hope, our dream. Deep inside, down so deep that our wives and mothers and sisters and women friends can hardly imagine it, we want to be godly men. We know that God is not finished with us yet. And perhaps some of us are on the brink of making a very stupid, life-changing decision. Some of us may have already crossed that line, and we may be wondering what to do now. For example, if we have blown it through sexual sin, does that mean God is through with us forever?

A Peek Behind the Curtain

The story of Jesus and Peter gives us a peek behind the scenes of history. For just a moment the veil is lifted, the curtain parted, and we catch a glimpse of amazing things that are normally off-limits to human beings. In these words of Jesus we learn about a high-level conference between God and Satan. If the thought sounds strange to you, as it does to me, let me remind you that it is not unparalleled. Job chapter 1 records a similar scene. There, we read that one day, when the angels presented themselves to the Lord, Satan came with them. But there is a significant difference between the accounts about Job and Peter. In Job 1 it is God who suggests Job as a suitable target for the devil; in Luke 22, it is Satan himself who desires to "sift" Peter like wheat.

I am reminded of a book written many years ago by Donald Grey Barnhouse titled *The Invisible War*. In that monumental book, Dr. Barnhouse traced the long war between good and evil, light and darkness, the angels and the demons, and ultimately, between God and Satan. He pointed out that Satan's goal all along has been to derail, delay, and destroy God's plan through any means possible. Many of these attacks came during and around the cross because that was the climactic moment when Satan was decisively defeated.

From Peter's story we learn an important truth that helps us understand our own temptations better. *Let us never forget that Satan wants something from us in the moment of temptation, and so does God!* The one wants to destroy us, and the other wants to deliver us. In Peter's case, we see how Satan's temporary victory in Peter's life leads to a much greater victory for God in the end. So it is for us as well. Our defeats, bitter as they are, can lead to great spiritual victories.

The Scene Played Out

Satan's Desire

Jesus clearly stated what was happening when He said, "Simon, Simon, Satan has asked to sift you as wheat" (Luke 22:31). The word translated "has asked" is a bit stronger than that in the Greek. It refers to a strong demand. Satan had set his eyes on Peter and was determined to bring him down by any means possible.

I find it comforting that Satan must ask God's permission before touching any of His children. Sometimes Christians become frozen in fear because they have given Satan too much credit. Sometimes we talk as if Satan were a kind of "junior god," almost God but not quite, as if he has, say, 90 percent of God's power, 90 percent of His wisdom, and so on. But that is quite different from the biblical picture. Satan is always revealed as a creature of great power and cunning who is nevertheless first and always a *created* being. He has no power independent of God. He can only do what God permits him to do. As Martin Luther put it, the devil is "God's devil." One Puritan writer called him "God's lapdog." Surely this is more biblical than viewing him as some evil force equal with God. If he were God's equal, he wouldn't have had to ask permission before attacking Peter.

I should note also that the "you" in Luke 22:31 is plural. Satan wanted to destroy all the apostles, but he specifically targeted Peter. This makes sense when you think about it: Satan goes after spiritual leaders. He starts at the top because he knows that if he can knock off the leader, others will no doubt fall in short order. That's why the devil goes after leaders— elders, pastors, deacons, teachers, and parents.

Satan's desire is to "sift" God's people by putting them under such pressure that they will give way and their faith be proved spurious. If that is the case, why would God permit His children to be put in such a bad position? So that

He can prove that even under severe pressure, we can survive if we depend wholly upon His grace.

Christ's Prayer

After warning Peter, Jesus added, "I have prayed for you, Simon, that your faith may not fail" (Luke 22:32). These simple words contain amazing reservoirs of truth. *First, they tell us that Christ knew in advance everything that Peter was about to do.* He knew about the denials, the cursing, the repeated lies Peter was about to tell; and He knew about the bitter tears Peter would shed when he saw Christ taken away in judgment. Even more than that, Jesus knew that one day Peter would become a mighty preacher of the gospel. He saw it all—the pride, the reckless boasting, the shameful denials, the broken heart, the deep repentance, and the new resolve to serve the Lord. He saw it all before any of it had happened. He saw it before Peter knew anything about it.

Second, Christ's response to Peter's fall was to pray for him. Hebrews 7:25 tells us that Christ prays for us in heaven, and it is because of His prayers that we are saved completely. In a deep sense our salvation depends on the moment-by-moment prayers of Jesus for His people—not in general or by groups, but one by one He prays for us: "Lord, there's Mike and I know he is struggling. Help him to stay strong. Sharon needs your help, Father. Julio is about to fall into temptation. Don't let him be utterly destroyed. Megan wants to do right. Help her to have the courage she needs." What an awesome thought—that the Son of God prays for us! Without His prayers, we would never make it.

Third, Christ did not pray for Peter to be removed from temptation. Instead, Jesus prayed that Peter, in the midst of his shame, would not lose his faith altogether. "Father, Satan wants to sift him to destroy him altogether. Please don't let that happen."

What a revelation this is of God's purposes for you and me! This explains so much about why we go through hard times. Many times God intends that we should face the truth of our own personal failures so that our trust might be in Him alone.

Peter's Fall and Restoration

Jesus closed with this admonishment: "And when you have turned back, strengthen your brothers" (Luke 22:32). Was Peter a believer? Yes, of course, and he had been a believer from the day he left all to follow Christ. But his soon-to-be shocking failure would be the means God used to radically change his life.

Note the little word "when." What a word of grace that is! Christ knew all about Peter's coming fall, but more than that, he saw that Peter would one day return to the Lord and be stronger than ever. Theologians call this the doctrine of the perseverance of the saints. It means that those who have trusted Christ will maintain their faith to the end. Years ago I heard someone rephrase the doctrine this way. He called it the doctrine of the perseverance of God and the preservation of the saints. *Because God perseveres with us, we are preserved safe through our many trials.* Do we persevere? Yes, but only because God first perseveres with us. If He didn't, we never would and never could.

I've noticed two encouraging facts about the way Jesus treated Peter: 1) *He never criticized him,* and 2) *He never gave up on him.* Jesus knew about Peter's denial long before it happened. He knew what Peter would do, He knew how Peter would react, and He knew the kind of man Peter would be afterward. That's why He said, *"When* you have turned back...." Not *if,* but *when!* He knew that Peter's heart was good; He knew that after his terrible sin he would return to the Lord. Isn't that wonderful? *Jesus had more faith in Peter than Peter had in Jesus.* He knew that Peter had important work to do—"strengthen your brothers"—but it couldn't happen without his fall and his restoration to the Lord. It had to happen that way, so that Peter might be more effective for Christ.

There is an important principle at work here. A bone that is broken often becomes stronger after it is healed. Something in the healing process actually makes the break point stronger than it was before. The same is true of a rope that breaks. In the hands of a master splicer, the rope once repaired becomes stronger than it was before.

And the same thing is true of our failures. *God can touch our broken places and make us stronger than we were before.* Though we fall and fall and fall, and though our faces are covered with the muck and grime of bitter defeat, by God's grace we can rise from the field of defeat to march on to new victory.

That's what happened to Peter. His guilt was turned into grace; his shame into sympathy; his failure into faithfulness.

Why God Allows Us to Fail

I have already noted that Jesus knew about Peter's fall and even predicted it, but He never tried to prevent it. This raises an interesting question: If God knows about our failures even before we fail, why doesn't He stop us? Why does He let us go headlong over the cliff? Here are three possible answers.

1. *To show us the depth of our sin*

As long as we stand on top of the cliff, we can brag about our goodness, but when we are lying at the bottom, bruised and broken, we are forced to admit the truth about ourselves. I believe this explains what happened to Peter and what often happens to us. Satan often attacks us at the point of our strength, not the point of our weakness. If you had asked Peter six hours earlier to name his strong points, no doubt he would have listed boldness and courage right at the top. He would have said, "Sometimes I put my foot in my mouth, but at least I'm not afraid to speak up. Jesus knows that I'll always be there when He needs me."

But when Satan attacked, it came so suddenly, so swiftly, so unexpectedly that the bold apostle turned to butter. In the moment of crisis, Peter failed at the very point where he pledged to be eternally faithful. Should this surprise us? After all, why should Satan attack only at the point of our self-perceived weakness? *If you know you have a weakness, that's the very area you will guard most carefully.* If you know you have a problem with anger or with laziness or with lust or with gluttony, will you not be on your guard lest you fall? But it is not so with your strengths. You tend to take those areas for granted. You say, "That's not a problem for me. I have other problems, but that area is not really a temptation at all."

Watch out! Put up the red flag! There is danger ahead. When a person takes any area of life for granted, that's the one area Satan is most likely to attack. Why? Because that's the one area where you aren't expecting his attack.

It happened to Peter, and it will happen to you and me sooner or later.

2. *To purge us from pride*

I don't think Peter ever forgot that sad night when he denied the Lord. Never again would he boastfully claim to be more courageous than the other apostles. So it is with all of us. Our failures are like Jacob's limp. They serve as a perpetual reminder and a guard against overwhelming pride. It is a good thing that the Lord allows this to happen to us. By falling flat on our faces, we are forced to admit that without the Lord we can do nothing but fail. The quicker we learn that (and we never learn it completely), the better off we will be. Failure never seems to be a good thing when it happens, but if it ends up stripping away our self-confidence, then something good has come from our failure.

Years ago at a crucial moment in my life I lost my temper and said some things to some dear friends that I came later to deeply regret. The volcanic eruption of evil words both frightened and surprised me. Where had all that anger come from? A month later while attending a conference in another state, I happened to meet a man who was to become a close personal friend. One night we stayed up late and I told, in exhaustive detail, the story of my personal explosion. As I told it, I got angry all over again. My friend listened to the whole sordid tale and then he spoke. "Ray, you are a lucky man. What happened to you was a sign of God's grace." I was baffled by his words. Had he missed the point of my story? But he knew me better than I knew myself. "God has shown you His grace by allowing you to lose your temper like that."

But how could losing my temper be an act of God's grace? He continued, "For many years you've had the image of a man completely in control of his life. You appear on the outside to be laid back. People who don't know you well think that you don't have a worry in the world. And you've cultivated that image because it makes you popular and easy to like. But the truth is far different. There's a seething cauldron inside you that you've managed to keep a lid on for a long time. But that night, the lid came off. Before that night, if anyone had said, 'Do you have a temper?' you would have laughed and said, 'Not really.' You can't say that anymore."

Then he went on to explain a fundamental truth about the Christian life. "As we grow in Christ, most of us come to the place where we think there are some sins we just won't commit. Maybe we don't say it out loud, but in our hearts we think, 'I would never do that.' That's what happened to you and your temper. You covered yours for so long that you thought it had gone away. But it was there, like a snake coiled in the grass, waiting for the chance to strike."

He concluded with these penetrating words: "That night, God pulled back the cover and let the world see the depravity within your own heart. From now on, whenever you stand up and speak, you can never say, 'I don't have a temper,' because you do. God let you say those terrible things to your friends so that you could never again pretend to be something that you are not. That's the grace of God at work in your life." I believe every word my friend said was absolutely true. God let me fail in the moment of crisis, and in so doing, He showed me a part of myself I had never seen before.

That's what God did for Peter. Never again would Peter stand up and boast about his courage. In the future, he would talk about the necessity for humility instead.

3. *To prepare us for a greater work we must do*

For some reason we can't fully understand, Peter *had* to fall so that God could raise him back up again. The falling part was Peter's own doing; the raising up came by the gracious hand of the Lord. But there is no getting up without falling down first. Even so, our failures qualify us to minister to others we could never otherwise reach. I have seen divorced people who have experienced God's grace greatly used to help others going through that same heartbreak. The same is true of those once trapped by drug and alcohol addiction, sexual sin, and those who have served time in prison. God sent Chuck Colson to prison and used him to found Prison Fellowship. That principle should not surprise us in the least. If God is God, and if nothing is ever wasted in life, if even the worst moments and our deepest failures somehow play a part in God's plan for us, if that is true, then sometimes our failures become the springboard to reach others who are in pain from the same mistakes we have made. I know of ex-prostitutes who minister to friends who are still in "the profession." And women who have had abortions know how to minister to other women who have made the same mistake.

Now, none of this justifies sin in the least. Sin is still sinful, disobedience is always wrong, and when we arrogantly go our own way, we all pay a heavy price. But God's grace is so great that there is no sin we can commit that disqualifies us forever from helping others along the way. Our sin may remove us from positions of public influence (and often that is exactly what should happen), and we may suffer and our family may suffer with us. Yet in the end, if we follow the Lord, we will discover that He never intended to destroy us. Rather, He only meant to purge us, to humble us, and to prepare us to serve Him in a new way.

God often uses broken people to accomplish great things. If you doubt this, let's do a roll call of broken saints!

Noah, who got drunk

Abraham, who lied about his wife

Jacob, who was a deceiver

Moses, who murdered an Egyptian

Rahab, who was a harlot

David, who was an adulterer

Paul, who persecuted the church

Peter, who denied Christ

Here is an amazing thought to ponder: *Peter did much more for Jesus Christ after his fall than he did before.* Before his fall, he was loud, boisterous, and unreliable; afterward, he became a flaming preacher of the gospel. Before, he was a big talker; afterward, he talked only of what Jesus Christ could do for others. He was the same man, but he was different. *He was still Peter through and through, but he had been sifted by Satan, and as a result of the sifting, the chaff of his life had been blown away.*

This is what Peter lost in his failure:

His vanity

His pride

His self-confidence

His rash impulsiveness

His unreliability

And this is what Peter gained after his restoration:

Humility

New confidence in God

Tested courage

A new determination to serve Jesus Christ

A willingness to use his experience to help others

The things Peter lost he didn't really need; the things Peter gained couldn't have come any other way. In the same way, God redeems our mistakes by removing the things that brought us down and replacing them with the qualities He can use.

Lessons from Our Brokenness

Last night a friend dropped by for a visit. During our conversation, he mentioned a family in our church going through a hard time. I commented to my friend that if we knew the naked truth about every person in our congregation, we'd all run away screaming. I, for one, am glad I don't know the truth about everyone. Let's face it: We're all broken people. Some of us just hide our brokenness better than others. There's a little bit of Peter in all of us, and that's why Peter's story speaks to all of us.

What should we learn from Christ's words to Peter?

a. *The value of humility.* If Christ's handpicked number one man could succumb to denying Him, then none of us can claim to be beyond temptation. Peter wasn't a bad man, but he was weak and he didn't realize how weak he was until it was too late. A little humility is always in order. You're not as hot as you think you are...and neither am I.

b. *The need for patience with each other.* Sometimes we act surprised when our Christian friends disappoint us. Perhaps we should be surprised when they don't. Certainly we'd all be happier if we lowered our expectations to a level consistent with reality. Even on our best days we will still sin and disappoint ourselves and others. It behooves us all to cut each other a little bit of slack.

c. *The magnificence of God's grace.* None of us really understands God's grace. This is the hardest of all Christian doctrines to grasp because it goes against our deeply felt need to prove ourselves worthy. Grace says, "You aren't worthy, but I love you anyway." That's hard to hear and hard to believe—and sometimes very hard to extend to other Christians. Meditate on God's grace. Think about it. Rest in it. Rejoice in it. Talk about it. Share it. Sing it.

One final point: Where did Peter's story come from? How did it get in the Bible? Who told this story in the first place? It could only have come from Peter. No one else was there to tell what happened. We wouldn't have. We hide our mistakes to make sure no one finds out about them. Not Peter. Once he was restored, he couldn't stop talking about what Jesus had done for him.

A Call to Move Forward

Several years ago the Lord gave me a series of simple statements that I call the First Law of Spiritual Progress.

I CAN'T GO BACK

I CAN'T STAY HERE

I MUST GO FORWARD

You can't go back to the past—not to relive the good times or to undo the mistakes you've made. But you can't stay where you are, either. *Life is a river that flows endlessly onward.* It matters not whether you are happy in your present situation or whether you seek deliverance from it. You can't stay where you are forever. The only way to go is forward. When you are tempted to despair, remember that you can't go back, you can't stay where you are, but by God's grace, you *can* move forward one step at a time.

Peter still speaks to us today. "If you think you've fallen short, if you feel like you've denied Him, look at what happened to me." Do not despair. God still loves you, and He loves you so much that it doesn't matter what you've done. If God can forgive Peter, He can forgive anybody. He loves you, He always has, and He always will.

One friend told me she found hope because, like Peter, she had made her share of mistakes. I replied that people with a past would find comfort in his story. As true as that is, it's also true that we all have "a past" and therefore we all stand in Peter's shoes—greatly loved, capable of foolish choices, and yet redeemed and redeemable for greater things in the future. Someone has said that the difference between a saint and a sinner is that a saint has a past and a sinner has a future. Both parts of that statement are true.

The God who forgives our past and our present has already made provisions to forgive our future as well. What an awesome thought that is. You who read these words, take heart. You may be heading for a fall and you don't know it yet. Take heart—the God who loves you enough to let you fall will Himself pick you back up again.

Here is more good news for all of us: God specializes in taking what is broken and putting it back together again. The church is a collection of broken people who have discovered God's grace and who tell other broken people where they can discover that grace. The world takes broken things and throws them away. God puts them back together again. If you are broken, do not despair. Keep believing, and hang on to Jesus. In the end you will be like Peter— restored, renewed, and ready to serve the Lord again.

CHAPTER 8

His Faithfulness to the Doubting

D o you believe in miracles? Do you believe in honest-to-goodness, old-fashioned acts of God? Most of us, I suppose, would immediately answer, "Yes, I believe in miracles." And I would say the same. If I were to ask you how many miracles you have ever seen, you would prob-ably say, "Oh, I don't know. I think all of life is a miracle." Or you might say, "I finished my income tax forms last night and that's a miracle."

Both of those statements are examples of how we can use the word *miracle,* but they are not what I mean when I say, "Do you believe in miracles?" I'm not thinking about the surprising events of life or difficult projects finally completed. By *miracle,* I mean those contrary-to-human-possibility events that have no natural explanation. "Oh," you say, "That kind of miracle. Sure, I believe in that kind of miracle." But now you are probably a little more uncer-tain. By definition, that kind of miracle doesn't happen every day. They happen very rarely, in fact. When they do happen, they are often hard to believe—partly because they don't happen very often and partly because we can't explain them. Even in the Bible that kind of miracle is not an every-day occurrence.

The resurrection of Jesus is that kind of miracle. It is totally unexplainable by any human or natural means. That may be why we don't talk about it very much. We're not sure how it happened. The crucifixion we can understand; the resurrection is another matter. Here's the proof: Lots of people wear little crosses around their necks. You don't see many people wearing little empty tombs.

So I ask the question again: Do you believe in miracles? Do you believe in the greatest miracle of all—the resurrection of Jesus Christ? If you answer, "No" or, "I'm not sure," you are in good company. There are many people today who aren't sure whether they believe it or not. And there were many people on the first Easter Sunday who weren't sure, either. Folks like Peter, James, John, Matthew, Bartholomew, Simon the Zealot, and a man whose name has become synonymous with doubt—Thomas. Doubting Thomas.

Was Thomas Really a Doubter?

In this chapter I want to take a closer look at Thomas because I think he's gotten a bit of a bum rap. Upon studying his story, his doubt seems very understandable to me. I think a consideration of all the evidence will help us see him in a different light. Let's see what we can learn about Thomas.

He Was a Twin

The Bible doesn't tell us much about Thomas. We don't know anything about where he comes from or what he did before becoming a disciple. We do have a little clue about his family. When you read about Thomas, he is usually introduced this way: "Thomas who was called Didymus." Now that doesn't mean anything to us, but the original readers recognized it immediately. The name "Thomas" comes from the Aramaic word for *twin*. And "Didymus" is the Greek word for *twin*. Thomas had a twin brother or sister, and "Twin" was his nickname. In the early church there was quite a bit of speculation about who the other twin might be. Some have suggested Matthew, but no one knows for sure.

He Possessed Enormous Courage

It's unfortunate that Thomas is remembered solely in a negative light. There is more to this man than doubt. He first steps onto the stage of biblical history in John 11. Lazarus had died in Bethany—a suburb of Jerusalem. Jesus and the disciples are in the region of Jericho when they get the word. When Jesus decides to go to Bethany, His disciples remind him that the last time He went near Jerusalem, the Jewish religious leaders tried to stone Him to death. It would be suicidal to go back. Jesus decides to go anyway. But the disciples were unconvinced. At that point, Thomas speaks up and says, "Let us go also, that we may die with him" (John 11:16). It is a brief statement that reveals enormous courage. Thomas agreed that the Jewish leaders would probably kill Jesus if He went back to Jerusalem. Events would soon prove him correct. But what can you say about a man who says, "If they kill him, they'll have to kill me, too?" It takes a real man to say that. Thomas shows love, loyalty, despair, sacrifice, and total commitment. It may just be that Thomas understood better than any other disciple what was about to happen. And that brave statement—if you think about it—may explain the doubts that arose later.

He Did Not Accept Easy Answers

John's Gospel mentions Thomas one other time before the crucifixion. It is late Thursday night in the Upper Room. Jesus has just washed the disciples' feet and given them the great command to love one another. Judas leaves the room

to do his dirty deed. The rest of the disciples crowd around
their Lord, knowing the end is not far away. To them—those
loyal men who had stood with Him up to now—Jesus said,

> Do not let your hearts be troubled. Trust in God;
> trust also in me. In my Father's house are many
> rooms; if it were not so, I would have told you. I
> am going there to prepare a place for you. And if
> I go and prepare a place for you, I will come back
> and take you to be with me that you also may be
> where I am. You know the way to the place I am
> going (John 14:1-4).

Thomas has been listening quietly, intently, carefully. All
this talk of coming and going is too much for him. It seems
vague and mysterious. In a moment of great honesty he
blurts out, "Lord, we don't know where you are going, so
how can we know the way?" (John 14:5). Those are the
words of a totally honest man. The rest of the disciples were
just as perplexed, but only Thomas dared to speak out. We
all know people like that—if they don't understand, they
won't let it pass. They keep asking until it makes sense.
That's Thomas. And that's a second key to his personality.
He was an independent thinker, a thoughtful man, not easily
stampeded. He wouldn't make a confession of faith unless
he deeply believed it to be true. Let others have a glib, easy
faith that comes without reflection and deep thought. Not
Thomas. His was a faith won through the agony of personal
struggle.

He Was Fully Devoted to Jesus Christ

So the picture we have of Thomas on the eve of the crucifixion is this: He is a brave man, intensely loyal and deeply
committed to Jesus. If need be, he is ready to lay down his
own life. He is no doubt inclined to look somewhat on the
dark side of life. He is completely honest about his doubts,

confusion, and fears. And he won't be satisfied with second-hand answers.

Would We Have Doubted?

We tend to forget what it was like on that first Easter morning. It is worth asking ourselves: If we had been there, would we have believed or would we have doubted? Or to put the question another way, What would it take to convince you that someone you loved had come back to life after being dead three days? Suppose it was a close friend or family member and you had watched them die. What would it take to convince you? Or is there any way you could be convinced? Rising from the dead is not a common thing. At best, it hasn't happened for centuries. If we had been there in Jerusalem with Matthew, James, and John, would we have believed those strange rumors that Sunday morning? In answering that question, it helps to remember how those who knew Jesus best reacted to the news of His resurrection.

None of the Disciples Believed at First

Very simply, they were not expecting a resurrection. Now it's true that Jesus had predicted that He would be put to death and then raised to life. But His followers did not understand that. A resurrection was the farthest thing from their minds. Forget Jesus' predictions. Forget all that brave talk. They had given up. Who really expected a resurrection on that Sunday morning? Not the disciples. It was the Jewish leaders who persuaded the Romans to seal the tomb. The enemies of Jesus feared something might happen. By contrast, Jesus' friends weren't expecting anything.

Mark 16 says that the women who came to Jesus' tomb on Sunday morning came to anoint His body. That was part of the embalming process. In the confusion of trying to get the body into the tomb before sundown on Friday, spices had been placed on Jesus' body, but not the ointment. The women came to finish embalming His body. What did they find when they got there? The stone rolled away, and an empty tomb. All four Gospels agree on this fact. The women did not have the slightest idea what had happened. They weren't looking for a resurrection.

Mark says that even after the angel explained what had happened, they fled from the tomb trembling and afraid (Mark 16:8). John says that even Mary thought someone had stolen the body (John 20:2). Luke adds that when the women came and told the apostles what the angel had said, "They did not believe the women, because their words seemed to them like nonsense" (Luke 24:11). Nonsense? Of course. No one rises from the dead—not after three days. Not after being scourged. Not after hanging on a cross for six hours. Not after having a sword thrust in His side. Not after being covered with 100 pounds of spices and wrapped in a burial cloth. Not after being sealed in a tomb. No, the odds are against it. It was impossible. He was a nice man. He meant well. We all loved Him. We walked with Him as He told those wonderful stories. And, oh, the miracles He did. We laughed when He told off the Pharisees. How about that time when He did that miracle with the fishes and the loaves? We thought that was great.

Sure, He said He would rise again. We all believed it. He even believed it. He had never been wrong before. Why not? He said He was the Son of God. We're sure going to miss Him. Wouldn't it have been great if He had pulled it off? Nobody would believe it. What a party we'd have. And Mark says, "When they heard that Jesus was alive...they did not believe it" (Mark 16:11). Who could blame them? If you had been there, would you have believed it?

Thomas Was Not Present

John tells us that Thomas was not present on that Sunday evening when Jesus suddenly appeared in their midst (John 20:19-25). The Bible doesn't say why, but I think I know. There are basically two different ways people respond to sorrow and tragedy. Some seek solace in the company of their friends. They want people around to help them talk it out. Others prefer to be alone with their thoughts. Such was Thomas. If it is true that Thomas realized more than the others what was going to happen in Jerusalem, then it may also be true that he was more deeply hurt. He was not with the other disciples because his heart had been crushed. Everything he had he had given to Jesus, and Jesus had died. He still loved, still cared, still wanted to believe, but his heart was broken. He was not a bad man nor was his doubt sinful. Deep inside he wanted to believe. Don't put him down too hard. We've all been in the same place.

If you wish to call Thomas a doubter, please do not make him out an unbeliever. Some have tried to place him in the company of the skeptics. He does not belong there. Thomas is definitely not a skeptic or a rationalist. His doubts come from devotion to Christ. *There is no doubt like the doubt of a broken heart.* It's one thing to doubt the virgin birth in a classroom setting. It is something else again to lose someone you love and wonder if there is still a God in heaven.

Thomas Was Not a Skeptic

There are two kinds of doubters in the realm of spiritual truth. There are the hard-boiled rationalists who say, "I don't believe it, and there's nothing that will make me believe it." Such people enjoy their doubt, talk about it, laugh about it, and get angry when they are refuted. A person like that is not looking for answers; he's looking for an argument. He counts the difficulties, seizes objections, and looks for loop-holes. The Pharisees were in that category. When they asked Jesus for a sign, He refused, calling them "a wicked and adulterous generation" (Matthew 16:1-4).

Thomas' Doubt Sprang from a Broken Heart

But there is another kind of doubter—the person who says, "I don't believe, but I'm willing to believe if I can see for myself." Thomas fits this category. He is not an unbe-lieving skeptic; he is a wounded believer. Remember, Thomas didn't doubt the miraculous in general. He had seen many of Jesus' greatest miracles. But this one was too big to take someone else's word for it. He had to see it to believe it. And who could blame him?

Thomas Was Not Unwilling to Believe, but Unable

No one wanted to believe more than Thomas. But he had seen too much, he knew too much; all the facts pointed in one direction. Before Thomas would believe, he had to personally see Jesus. And he had to be sure it was Jesus—not some dream or vision. He had to be sure it was the same Jesus he saw die. That's why he couldn't just take the word of the disciples. Not on something like this. He was not unwilling to believe, but unable.

Some people are satisfied with the testimony of others. Some are not. Thomas was not. Did he doubt the truthful-ness of the others? No, he knew they believed they had seen Jesus. But that wasn't enough. Lots of people think they see things. Thomas couldn't get rid of the suspicion that they had seen a ghost. He could not live with a secondhand faith. He had to see for himself. When he said, "Unless I touch his wounds, I will not believe," there is much more than doubt. There is love, and sorrow, and pain, and a tiny grain of hope. Thomas stands for all time as the one man who most desperately wanted to believe, if only he could be sure. Can you blame him? Would you have been any different?

Jesus Invited Thomas to See for Himself

After all these years, Thomas has gotten a bad reputation. Doubting Thomas, we call him. We tend to look down on him. But not Jesus. Eight days later, Jesus appeared to the disciples a second time. This time, Thomas was with them. Jesus spoke to him as to one whose faith was weak, not to one who had an evil heart. He said, "Put your finger here; see my hands. Reach out your hand and put it into my side. Stop doubting and believe" (John 20:27). It's worth noting that Jesus knew all about Thomas' doubts. Jesus knew the raging sea within Thomas' heart. And He came just so Thomas could be sure. Jesus didn't put him down. He said, "Go ahead, all you who wonder if it is true. See for yourself. Stop doubting and believe." Here is the wonderful truth: *Doubters are welcome at the empty tomb.*

Do you believe in miracles? If you answer, "No" or, "I'm not sure," then welcome. It's okay to be an honest doubter. If you came that way and want to leave that way, it's okay. When you're ready, He'll be there waiting for you. Sometimes we act as if all doubt is sinful and that people with doubts are not welcome in church. And sometimes we try to pretend that Christians have everything sewn up, all the questions answered, and that we never have doubts. That attitude is both sad and wrong. We all have our doubts and most of us would be healthier if we admitted that fact. Our Lord welcomes every sincere person and invites the doubters to check out the evidence for themselves.

This story also teaches us that Christianity is based on verifiable evidence. *Christ never asks us to believe for no reason at all.* He told Thomas to check out the evidence and come to his own conclusion. He makes the same invitation to you and to me. Ours is a skeptical, jaded generation that has learned to question everything. We've been lied to by people in authority and misled so often by the media and by Hollywood that we automatically doubt any claims to absolute truth. When Christians declare that Christ is risen from the dead, we shouldn't be surprised when someone says, "Oh yeah? I saw that on the David Copperfield special the other night." Over the centuries unbelievers have propounded many theories to explain away the bodily resurrection of Jesus: That Jesus didn't really die, He just passed out and revived in the tomb; that the women went to the wrong tomb; that someone stole the body—the Romans, the Jews, the disciples; that Jesus somehow faked His own death and then pretended to come back from the dead; that the disciples had a mass hallucination and imagined that Jesus rose from the dead; that Jesus rose spiritually while His body remained in the tomb; that the early church concocted the whole story. Even today there are those who still cling to these outmoded, discredited ideas. We say to everyone what Jesus said to Thomas: "Come and see for yourself. Check out the evidence. Read the story with an open heart and an open mind. Stop doubting and believe." We believe that when all the evidence has been fairly evaluated, the only possible conclusion is that on Good Friday Jesus died and was buried and on Easter Sunday morning He rose from the dead. *The entire Christian faith hangs on this one fact: Jesus rose from the dead—literally, physically, bodily, visibly.*

During the turbulent days following the French Revolution, a man decided to start his own religion but found that he had difficulty attracting new converts. When he asked for advice, a friend told him this: "To ensure success for your new religion, all you need to do is have yourself crucified and then rise from the dead on the third day." His religion disappeared because he was unable to follow that advice. Jesus is the only person in history who has ever met that qualification.

Are There Benefits to Doubt?

Doubt does have its uses. Deep doubt is often the prelude to an even deeper faith. I love the way Frederick Buechner expresses it: "Whether your faith is that there is a God or that there is not a God, if you don't have any doubts you are either kidding yourself or asleep. Doubts are the ants in the pants of faith. They keep it awake and moving." It is a wonderful truth that the greatest doubters often become the strongest believers. And the honest doubts— once resolved—often become the bedrock of an unshakeable faith. It has been said that no truth is so strongly believed as that which you once doubted. In the history of the Christian church, the greatest doubters have often become the strongest believers. That's why the story of Thomas is in the Bible—so that honest doubters might be encouraged to bring their honest doubts to the empty tomb. Thomas did, and his doubts were washed away by the person of Jesus Christ—alive from the dead.

Have You Moved from Doubt to Faith?

All that God asks is that men be consistent with themselves. He asks that you give the resurrection story the same treatment you give to any other story. Sift the evidence, judge the record, and come to a conclusion. It's all right to doubt, but don't let your doubts keep you away. Come to the empty tomb and see for yourself. When Thomas saw Jesus, he fell at his feet and exclaimed, "My Lord and my God" (John 20:28). That stands as the greatest testimony given by any of the apostles. It is the climax of John's Gospel. And it came from the man who had the strongest doubts.

Where do we fit in? After all, Jesus has gone back to heaven. We don't have the same opportunity Thomas had of seeing the Lord Jesus face to face. What do we do with our doubts? Jesus has a word for us, too. "Blessed are those who have not seen and yet have believed" (John 20:29). There are those who say that the resurrection of Christ is not important, that what matters is that Jesus lives in our hearts. But if Jesus is still in the tomb, He is not living in our hearts. "If Christ has not been raised, your faith is futile; you are still in your sins" (1 Corinthians 15:17). Too many people, including some Christians, approach faith like the boy who said, "Faith is believing what you know is not true." Wrong! *Our faith is founded on the facts of history.* If any atheist or Buddhist or Hindu or materialist or Muslim or anyone else had been standing in that same room, he would have seen what Thomas saw. He would have seen Jesus because Jesus Christ was really there—alive from the dead. If we had been there, we could have touched His scars with our own hands.

Yet we are not there. We are here, 2000 years have passed, and Jesus promises a special blessing to those of us who believe without seeing. If you are waiting for some sort of mathematical proof that Jesus rose from the dead, I can't give it to you. But the historical record is there for everyone to examine. It contains abundant evidence for those who choose to believe, and people who decide not to believe can always find reasons not to believe.

No one can remain neutral forever. You can bring your doubts to the empty tomb, but you have to make a choice. You cannot stay on the fence forever. Either you believe, or you don't. It's a wonderful day to make that choice. It's a great day to stop doubting and start believing.

You know that Jesus died. There is no doubt about that. You know He died for you. You know He rose from the dead. The question God is asking you is this: "What have *you* done with My Son?"

Jesus said, "Stop doubting and believe."

CHAPTER 9

His Faithfulness
to the Dying

I have been closely touched by death four times in my life. The first time occurred when I was a student in junior high school, during seventh grade. A friend of mine got sick on a Sunday morning and suddenly died. It shook me up pretty bad because I used to go over to his yard and wrestle with him. We'd go inside and sit on the sofa and read comic books. He'd come to my house sometimes and we'd fool around together. We were just typical good friends. And then he died.

Our entire school was dismissed on the day of his funeral. I walked into the crowded church sanctuary and saw the casket open in the front. I remember standing at the back of that crowded auditorium and seeing the outline of his face up above the edge of the coffin. He was the first dead person I had ever seen. I was too scared to go up for a closer look.

The second time was when my grandmother died while I was in college. She was in her eighties and had been sick for some time, so her death came as no surprise. I drove through the night from Chattanooga to Nashville to Memphis and down to Oxford to attend the funeral service. When family members took me in to see her, someone commented, "They did a good job, didn't they?" Outside, my relatives were standing around laughing, talking, joking, sipping drinks. Only one aunt seemed concerned at all. I remember that it seemed rather bizarre, drinking cocktails at a funeral home.

The third time was when my father died in 1974 from a bacterial infection that inflamed his liver. It all happened so suddenly. I had seen him in early October at a football game in Jackson, Mississippi. A few days later, my mom called with the news that Dad was sick, which surprised me because he was a surgeon who made other people better. I could hardly ever remember him being sick. They took him to Birmingham, where he had surgery. There is a two-week period at the end of October that is a blur in my mind. I know that my bride and I (we had been married less than three months) made several trips from Dallas to Birmingham to see him. The last time I saw him, he was going in and out of a coma and didn't recognize me. He died soon after that.

No other event has ever affected my life like the death of my dad. It took me a long time to come to grips with what had happened. When I first wrote the previous sentence, I used the phrase "get over it," but that doesn't seem right, even after almost three decades. While I have finally come to accept that my father is gone, I still miss him greatly and would give anything to see him once again, if only for an hour or two. Even now, I find it hard to put into words how his death affected me. Though I wouldn't have said it this way at the time, I think that as long as he was alive, I felt safe and protected. Once he was gone, I felt alone in the world. In some way that is hard to explain—the world has never seemed truly safe to me since he died.

The fourth time happened several years ago when my friend Gary Olson suddenly died. For years he was the head football coach of Oak Park-River Forest High School. He also served as an elder of the church I pastor in Oak Park. He and I were very close friends. He and his wife, Dawn, and my wife, Marlene, and I once took a vacation together to the Cheyenne Frontier Days in Cheyenne, Wyoming. Every Sunday morning, Gary would come to my office to pray with me before the first worship service. I can still hear his deep voice praying that God would give me "fresh oil" as I preached the Word. Although he was a man's man and stayed in great physical condition, he had an enlarged heart caused by a defective valve. He survived a very difficult surgery and seemed to be doing fine when one day he collapsed en route to the high school while working out. He was dead before they got him to the hospital.

Over 4000 people attended his wake. His death shook our community to the core and caused multitudes to consider their own relationship with God. When I gave the invitation at his funeral service, over 20 people stood up to publicly commit their lives to Jesus Christ. As I ponder the question "Why did this happen?" I realize that I don't really know why things happen the way they do. Of the four deaths I have mentioned, my grandmother's makes the most sense from a human perspective. But I don't know why my young friend died when he was only 12 or 13 years old. Why did my father die when he did? God has His reasons, but they are far beyond my meager understanding. The same is true of the death of Gary Olson. Looking around, I can see many lives that have been touched because of his untimely death. Undoubtedly there will be people in heaven who came to Christ as a result of the way Gary lived and died. But is that the full explanation for why things happened the way they did? The answer almost certainly is no. I rest content that at best I can grasp a tiny sliver of God's eternal purposes as they work themselves out in a fallen world where death still reigns.

Trusting in God

Some people have trouble dealing with unanswerable questions, but as I grow a bit older, I find myself taking comfort in how little I know about how the universe works. In the sad, sorrow-filled days after Gary died, I had a long conversation with the Lord. "So you think I made a mistake by taking Gary home to heaven?" the Lord seemed to say to me. "Yes, I think You made a mistake," I replied. The Lord didn't seem offended by that. He already knew how I felt about it. "So you think I should have asked your opinion before I made My decision?" "Yes, Lord, that's exactly how I feel, and frankly, I wouldn't have made that decision at all. I would have told You to go find someone else to take home to heaven." Again the Lord didn't seem bothered by my comments. "Ray, just keep this in mind: I did what I did for My own reasons. But I did it without consulting you so you would know that I take full responsibility for when and how Gary died."

That conversation, which was all in my mind yet seemed very real to me, was a great comfort to my soul. I find it easy to worship a God who can suddenly and without warning take home a mighty Christian like Gary Olson. I felt then and feel now that only an Almighty God would do something like that and feel no need to explain Himself before or after. In a sense, the mystery of it all ended up building my faith. After all, why would I want to worship a God I could fully understand? "How unsearchable are His judgments and unfathomable His ways" (Romans 11:33 NASB).

And why am I alive while someone else is dead? I faced that question several years ago when the pastor of a large church in Chicago died suddenly. I pastor Calvary Memorial Church, and he was the pastor of Calvary Church in another Chicago suburb. I had met him several times and respected him as a man of God. When I heard that he had died, I recalled these words of Scripture: "You sweep men away in the sleep of death; they are like the new grass of the morning—though in the morning it springs up new, by evening it is dry and withered" (Psalm 90:5-6). The next day someone told me that he had heard the pastor's death announced on a local radio station, but he had only heard the part where the announcer said that the pastor of Calvary Church had suddenly died. He assumed they were talking about me. And the thought arose, *It could have been me.* Why the other pastor and not me? I don't know the answer to that question.

Death makes us realize our mortality, our weakness. And it frightens us because we instinctively know that we too will someday die. Most of all, death makes us think. It makes us think about our own lives, about our priorities, about our goals, about ourselves. And we generally don't like to think about those things. So we avoid death at all costs. We avoid death because we don't want to think about life. But sometimes it is inescapable. Sometimes death is forced in front of our very eyes...and we have to think about life.

Growing in Faith

John 4:46-54 tells the story of a man whose son was dying. We do not know the precise nature of the son's illness except that he had a high fever and was near the point of death. We do not know the son's name or his age, but there is a hint in the text that he is not yet an adult. The mother is not mentioned in this story, but we can assume that she shared her husband's profound concern.

Considering a Deep-seated Fear

I believe this is every parent's deepest fear—that somehow, someday, in an accident or by illness or through some other means, our children will be taken from us.

Nothing seems more unnatural than the death of a child. It is a prospect so terrible that we can hardly think of it, much less speak of it in public. Having to bury one of our own children is a tragedy we silently pray we will never have to endure. But it does happen. J.C. Ryle pointed out that the first recorded death in the Bible was not of a father but of a son—when Cain killed Abel. And when the apostle Paul pointed out that death has come to "all men" (Romans 5:12), he didn't mean just grown-up men, he meant the entire human race—young and old alike, rich and poor, male and female. Death has come and will come to all of us sooner or later. But when death draws near to the young, it brings the parents to a moment of personal crisis.

This week I chatted on the phone with my brother, Alan, who is a physician in Tupelo, Mississippi. He commented that when your child is sick, you don't care about test results, Xrays, percentages, new medicines, research protocols, or anything like that. To quote my brother directly: "People just want to know one thing: 'Is my child going to be all right?'" Nothing else matters. Everything else is just details.

Progressing in the Stages of Faith

This story in John 4 tells about an important man who had an important conversation with Jesus. As a result, he received a most incredible miracle. What happened to his son was not due to luck or coincidence. His son was dying, and Jesus healed him. And the wonder of the story is that Jesus never met the child, and the child never met Jesus. It was a long-distance miracle recorded by the apostle John for our benefit.

This story also illustrates how faith grows in the human heart. None of us is born into God's family with our faith fully developed. We all go through various stages to arrive where God wants us to be. The text of John 4 reveals to us seven stages of faith. Let's take a look together to see how faith grows in the midst of desperate circumstances.

Stage 1: Crisis

"Once more he visited Cana in Galilee, where he had turned the water into wine. And there was a certain royal official whose son lay sick at Capernaum" (John 4:46).

Faith almost always starts in a crisis. When things are going well, it's easy to forget God, but when life tumbles in around us, we suddenly start looking to heaven for help. This story centers on a man who is called a "royal official." (Some translations use the word "nobleman.") The original Greek text uses a general term that means "one who serves the king." It almost certainly means that he was an official in the government of Herod Antipas, the Tetrarch of Galilee and Perea. No doubt he was rich, powerful, and influential. He was in the upper crust, a power broker, a man others feared and respected. He was accustomed to giving orders and having them carried out. In his own corner of the world, he had enormous authority because he answered to the king and the king answered to Caesar. If he wanted something, it was done for him. If he had a request, he had but to say it and his will would be done. People came to him to have their problems solved. But now he had a problem he couldn't solve.

Even the rich and powerful have their troubles. Behind every smiling face is a story of sadness and heartache. No matter how much money a person has, he will never reach the place where he is protected from trouble. Trouble comes alike to the rich and to the poor. An Arab proverb declares that "grief is a black camel that kneels at every tent."

As I have already said, we do not know the exact details of his son's sickness. We only know this: It broke the father's heart and consumed all his energy. This man who could do so much had no power to help his son. He watched day by day as his beloved child grew weaker and the fever raged without breaking. When his son cried, "Daddy, help me," there was nothing he could do. At night when his son could not see him, he wet his pillow with tears of anguish.

Little did this official know that this heavy burden was an "angel" in disguise. If his son had not been sick, he might never have met Jesus. God often uses trouble to focus our attention on Him. Through this sickness, God now has this man's undivided attention. I love the words of Bible teacher A.W. Pink: "It is well when trouble leads a man to God, instead of away from God. Affliction is one of God's medicines."

The doctors must have already done all they could do, and evidently they said, "There is no hope." In such a situation, desperate men take desperate steps. Desperate times call forth desperate measures.

What will this man do?

Stage 2: Humility

"When this man heard that Jesus had arrived in Galilee from Judea, he went to him" (John 4:47).

By this time Jesus had become well known in Galilee. Not long before, He had performed the amazing miracle of turning water into wine. Word had spread that this carpenter from Nazareth had the power to heal the sick. Multitudes came to Him with maladies of every kind, and it was said that He healed them all. And word of Jesus' healing ministry reached the little fishing village of Capernaum on the northern shore of the Sea of Galilee.

That brings us to the second stage of faith. When the nobleman heard that Jesus had come to Cana, he instantly decided to go see Him. The man's plan was simple. He would meet Jesus face to face, explain his son's sickness, and ask Jesus to come back to Capernaum so He could heal his son. He was a man of action, of forceful decision, of courage in the face of uncertainty. If there were any chance that this man called Jesus could help his boy, he would go to Jesus himself. Please note that at this point he didn't really know who Jesus was. Like the woman at the well (John 4:1-42), he would not have passed a test in theology, but he had heard about Jesus, and wondered if He could help his son.

Who can blame the nobleman? He loved his son and wanted him to be healed. His son meant more than the world to him. He could have sent his servants to Jesus. That would have been appropriate, but he came himself. He didn't know Jesus, had never met Him, knew only His reputation, and that was enough for this man. In going to meet Jesus, he risked everything, for he did not know how Jesus would receive him, and he knew his son could die while he was gone. He would not have left his son's side for any other reason. He left in the desperate hope that his son might be healed. He didn't know what would happen! But he went anyway. That's what faith does. It doesn't know the future, but it steps out anyway.

Capernaum is on the northern shore of the Sea of Galilee, while Cana is in a hilly area about 22 miles away. As the nobleman traveled those dusty roads, I imagine he rehearsed over and over again what he would say. I'm sure he made up his mind that he would do whatever it took to convince Jesus to come to his son's bedside. As a royal official, he was accustomed to having people come to him. But now he had to humble himself and go to Jesus, pleading for his son's life. In this desperate moment, his money and power meant nothing. His friends could not help him. He came with nothing to offer and with only a desperate plea for his beloved son.

Stage 3: Request

"And begged him to come and heal his son, who was close to death" (John 4:47).

The best prayer is born of desperation. People generally don't pray until there's a great need. Those who aren't needy often forget to pray. That's why people who are in hospitals call for pastors and chaplains. They don't want to die with burdens on their souls. They want to be healed, and if they cannot be healed, they want to make sure they are ready to meet God. When hard times come, we cling to God like a drowning man clings to a rope. In this case, desperation turned a powerful man into a beggar. The word "begged" in the original Greek text means "to beg repeatedly." I do not doubt that this powerful official got on his knees and begged Jesus to come and heal his son. Even a skeptic will pray at a time like this. There are no atheists in the emergency room. When all human props are taken away, we realize that only God can help us.

It appears that the official's request was very simple and very direct: He said, in essence, "O Jesus, come and heal my son!" That's all. No King James English, no long preliminaries, no formalities. He got right to the point.

- He knew what he wanted: Jesus to come with him.

- He knew what he needed: Healing for his son.

- He knew why he needed it: His son was near death.

Time was of the essence. "Jesus, you must come right now. My son may die at any moment, but I know You can heal him." There is something positive and something negative in what the father says. On one hand, he totally believes Jesus can heal his son. But his faith is defective because he thinks Jesus must be personally present for the miracle to happen. He believes that for Jesus to work a miracle in Capernaum, He can't stay in Cana. Jesus has got to travel the 22 miles back to Capernaum in order for his son to be healed. Now, the father can be forgiven making this assumption. Most of us probably would have thought the same way.

Note especially that the official didn't try to use his wealth or his power to persuade Jesus, and he didn't try to argue that he deserved special treatment. And he didn't say, "My son is popular and handsome and gifted." His son was dying. That was all he needed to mention.

Stage 4: Persistence

"'Unless you people see miraculous signs and wonders,' Jesus told him, 'you will never believe.' The royal official said, 'Sir, come down before my child dies'"* (John 4:48-49).

Jesus' answer is unexpected and appears to be almost rude. It's as if He is irritated and doesn't want to bother with this man's sick son. Jesus was putting this man's faith to the test. "Are you coming to Me just because you want a miracle, or do you really know who I am?" *The problem for many of us is not our desire for miracles, but our addiction to miracles.* And this explains why Jesus would not go to Capernaum and heal the son in person. If He went to Capernaum and performed the miracle there, it would attract a great crowd. They would follow Him as a miracle worker but they would not believe in Him as the Son of God from heaven. He didn't want to become some kind of carnival sideshow. He would have become popular, but He would not have been worshiped as the Lord from heaven.

Because we want to see signs, we put conditions on the Lord before we will believe in Him. We like to say, "Seeing is believing." That's backwards. First you believe, then you see. Faith must always come before the miracles. Miracles have no use except to point to Jesus. If we get miracles but don't fall in love with Jesus as a result, we've missed the whole point. What seemed to be a rebuke was really a spiritual challenge. Jesus was moving the official to a higher level of faith. We want proof, but God honors faith. Strange as it seems, Jesus was actually helping the man by refusing his first request. Could Jesus have gone to Capernaum?

Sure—no problem. But that would not have helped this man's faith.

I love the way this desperate man responds. He simply repeats his request. It's as if he's saying, "I don't know anything about this signs and wonders stuff, but I know You can heal my son." He would not be turned away. Note that...

> He called Christ "Sir" or "Lord"—a term of great respect.

> He knew he had a need—his son was dying.

> He knew Christ could meet that need—He could heal his son.

> He knew what he knew, and that's all that mattered.

And for all that, the father's faith was still immature. He not only made a request, he also told Jesus how to answer his prayer. He tried to tell God how to be God. And that brings us once again to an important truth: *He's God, and we're not.* Who has been the Lord's counselor? No one! Who gives Him advice? No one! Who can trace His path across the starry skies? No one! This man had faith and a plan. The faith was good, the plan wasn't so good. I will often tell people, "Do you want to make God laugh? Tell Him your plans!" There was nothing wrong with this man's plan; it just wasn't Jesus' plan. The Lord had something bigger and better in mind.

In the course of writing this chapter I came across a wonderful definition of faith. I don't know who said it, but it fits our story and it applies to all of us who face desperate circumstances: "Faith is confidence in God's faithfulness to me in an uncertain world, on an uncharted course, through an unknown future."

Stage 5: Obedience

"Jesus replied, 'You may go. Your son will live.' The man took Jesus at his word and departed" (John 4:50).

The man said, "Come down," and Jesus said, "Go!" That put the royal official in a hard place. I am sure I would have argued the point. "Jesus, You've got to go with me. You don't understand how sick my son is. I can't take a chance. If You come, I know You can heal him." But something gripped his heart in that moment. I think the Holy Spirit whispered in his heart, "You can trust the words of Jesus." And he did. There were two miracles that day. The first one was the healing of the son. The second was the healing in the heart of the nobleman. It must have been hard for him to leave Cana and make the journey back to Capernaum alone. He had nothing to go on but the words of Jesus: "Your son will live." This is pure faith. Simple faith. This is faith not in miracles, but in the word of the Lord.

Would we have gone so easily or would we have stayed to argue more with Jesus? I find it noteworthy that this man didn't ask for a token or a sign. After all, he didn't know what would happen. He had no outward proof that his son would live. But he left anyway. If he was wrong about this, then his son would soon be dead. He was risking his son's life on the bare words of Jesus Christ. He left without a written promise, and there were no visible angels to accompany him. He had nothing to lean on but the word of the Lord. He believed that what Jesus said, He would do. St. Augustine put it this way: "Faith is to believe what we do not see, and the reward of faith is to see what we believe." Very soon, this man would have the reward of his faith.

Stage 6: Confirmation

"While he was still on the way, his servants met him with the news that his boy was living. When he inquired as to the

*time when his son got better, they said to him, 'The fever left
him yesterday at the seventh hour.' Then the father realized
that this was the exact time at which Jesus had said to him,
'Your son will live'"* (John 4:51-52).

Now we come to the delightful portion of the story. As
the man made the journey home, I'm sure many thoughts
were running through his mind. He knew what Jesus had
said, and he probably believed it. Yet he also remembered
how sick his son was when he left. Could the words of Jesus
really be true? I'm sure he wondered how long it would take
his son to fully recover from his deadly fever.

As he walked along the road, he saw before him in the
distance a crowd of people coming his way. Whoever they
were, they seemed to be in a great hurry. As they got closer,
he heard shouts, and he realized they were his servants. For
a moment, his heart may have hesitated as he considered
what their coming must mean. Was it bad news? But
no…they were laughing and shouting and smiling.

"Master, we have good news. Master, your son lives!"
Then they surrounded him, and the party started right there
in the middle of the road. Cheering, laughing, dancing,
shouting, and the father weeping with joy.

"How did it happen? When? Tell me everything!" The
father wanted to know when his son started to get better.

The laughter increased. "Master, you don't understand.
He didn't *begin* to get better. He got better all at once. It's a
miracle!"

"But when did it happen?" he asked.

"At the seventh hour" (which would be 1:00 P.M.).

The father probably paused for a moment to think and
count the hours on his fingers. The first hour, the second
hour, the third hour, the fourth hour, the fifth hour, the sixth
hour, the seventh hour. Then it hit him. The seventh hour!
That was the very moment when Jesus said, "Go your way.
Your son lives." Jesus healed the boy in Capernaum even

though He was 22 miles away in Cana! And the boy was healed the very moment Jesus spoke to the father. This was not a coincidence. This was a flat-out miracle. And it proved that Jesus is the Lord of time and distance.

Stage 7: Commitment

"So he and all his household believed. This was the second miraculous sign that Jesus performed, having come from Judea to Galilee" (John 4:53-54).

There is one final stage in the development of this man's faith. Three different times he believed in Jesus, and each time, his faith moved to a higher level.

- He believed first when he came to Jesus in Cana— faith in Jesus' *miracles.*

- He believed again when he left to go home to his son—faith in Jesus' *word.*

- He believed ultimately when his son was healed— faith in *Jesus Himself.*

And he believed so fully that he swept his whole family and all his servants with him into the kingdom of God. He came, and they came with him! Here is an important word for fathers. Let the father believe, and the mother will believe, too. Let father and mother believe, and the children will believe, too. Let the family believe, and soon the relatives will believe. Thus does God's grace spread from one person to another.

I should add at this point that not every prayer for help is answered in the same way as this father's request. Not every child is healed in a miraculous way. Oswald Chambers speaks to this point: "Faith for my deliverance is not faith in God. Faith means, whether I am visibly delivered or not, I will stick to my belief that God is love. There are some things only learned in a fiery furnace."

Recognizing God's Involvement

What's particularly special about this story is that it clearly demonstrates the sovereign hand of God at work in people's lives. Though the father could not see it in advance, his son was brought to the point of death that the entire family might be brought to eternal life. Thus does God work through our adversity, our pain, our trials, and our sorrows. When we are in the midst of desperate circumstances, we see only our problems and we come as children begging for help: "Lord Jesus, come quickly. We need You. The world is falling apart, and only You can help us." And Jesus quietly says, "Go your way. Be in peace. I will take care of your problems." Will we have the faith to go in peace, trusting Him? When we do, we will discover that Jesus is as good as His word. And very often we will look back much later and say, "I didn't see it then. In my sorrow and sadness, I thought the Lord had forgotten me. I thought my prayers had been ignored. But now I see clearly that the Lord was there all the time. He answered in ways I did not expect. And if it had not been for the Lord, I would not have made it at all."

When it comes to God's work in our lives, many times we can see that a greater miracle has been wrought than the one we sought in the beginning. And so we learn again that His ways are not our ways. Give God enough time, and all will be made right. He will be vindicated in all things, and His Word will be proved true. Our part is to trust Him and to obey the light we have. Once we bring our problems to Him, we must then go our way and trust Him to do what He knows is best. This is true faith.

Learning from an Example

At the age of 44, Steve Meyer was diagnosed with Stage 4 mantle cell lymphoma. That's a form of cancer that eventually takes the life of almost everyone who has it. Not many people live more than five or six years after their diagnosis. For many months, Steve was given heavy-duty chemotherapy in a desperate attempt to beat back the cancer and save his life. Even though his hair fell out and he battled with great pain, he faithfully continued to come to church, week after week. The initial results from the chemotherapy were encouraging. Many of the tumors disappeared, and others shrank dramatically.

The next step in the treatment cycle called for Steve to undergo a very difficult bone marrow transplant in which the doctors harvested his stem cells, radiated his whole body to destroy all his bone marrow, then reinserted the stem cells, all the while hoping his body would be able to fight off infection while his immune system was temporarily disabled. Steve knew the risks and knew that he could undergo this kind of treatment only once because his body would not be able to endure it twice. The doctors made no guarantees. The cancer could come back even after the bone marrow transplant, but this was still the best chance for a cure.

A few days before Steve went into the hospital, I spoke with him on the phone and found him to be incredibly cheerful and filled with optimism about the future. He had committed his life into God's hands and was content to leave everything with the Lord. He had also joined an e-mail listserv of 600 patients around the world who have his kind of cancer. Someone wrote him saying they had just been diagnosed with mantle cell lymphoma, and that person wondered what to expect. Steve wrote an answer that is an eloquent statement of faith. With his permission, I am reproducing it here:

I am not happy to have this disease, nor is anyone who has it. Chemotherapy is not a refreshment, bone marrow transplants are less fun than going to the lake in the summer. And having one's life ripped apart by a disease that has historically killed all its victims is not my first choice.

On the other hand, when you are surrounded by people who love you, people who pray for you, people who bring you meals, send you cards, rake your leaves, cry with you, laugh with you, do your chores for you, shovel your snow all winter, cut your grass all summer, come over on Sunday to watch football with you, call you on the phone, pick up your medicine for you, drive you places when you can't, offer you their homes, offer support to your husband or wife, offer support to your kids, offer support to your healthy parents, offer support to your brothers and sisters, come over to keep you company, take you out to dinner, bring you books, CDs, tapes, loan you their laptop computer, offer their friendship and love....

When your kids tell you they love you again and again and again and cry at the thought of losing you, when your wife or husband tells you they love you even when you act like an idiot and they cry themselves to sleep at the thought of losing you, when you see tears in your parents' eyes at the thought of losing a child to this disease and they say "I wish it were me" and they mean it....

When people you've never met pray for you, send you mail, encourage you, meet you for dinner, when the doctor weeps for you because he wishes he could do more, when the pain gets so bad it takes away your breath, or you get so sick you think you're gonna die....

I'll tell you what I do. I thank God for my life just the way it is! I have had a good life, and I intend to live for many years to come. I plan on seeing my Becky grow up. Today she was the happiest little girl in the third grade, and so proud to read her grades one by one to her dad, who she has no doubt loves her with all of his heart. I plan to see my 12-year-old son's penmanship improve even if it takes forever, and someday he will beat me in chess. I plan to see my sophomore-in-college daughter someday grow up the rest of the way and get married and give me grandkids. I plan to see my parents finish their lives with their son alive, and I'll bury them when they die. I plan to see my beautiful wife grow old, get gray hair, and sag, so I can love her more then than I do now, and we can retire to Florida.

Did we all get a bad break? Yes.

Do we have a right to complain? A little.

Would I change my life if I could? Never.

I'm glad you asked the question, and I pray that you and everyone else with this disease gets cured, and as for those who have died from this disease, I plan to see them again. The quality of my life has never been better!

May God bless all those with mantle cell lymphoma and the loving caregivers and families.

Steve Meyer
Oak Park, Illinois

Over the phone, Steve told me the secret of his strong faith. It consists of a simple statement that goes right to the heart of the Christian faith: "If you know the Lord, you don't need to fear dying, because if you know the Lord, you're never really dead." What an amazing statement that is. It's exactly what Jesus meant when He said, "Whoever lives and believes in me will never die" (John 11:26).

What can you do with a man like that? You can't stop him. His faith is indestructible. The devil can't touch a man like that because the devil's ultimate weapon is the fear of death. If you aren't afraid to die, then the devil has no power over you.

Achieving What We've Wanted

For 29 years, Tom Landry was the head coach of the Dallas Cowboys. He was also a strong Christian and for many years was on the board of my alma mater, Dallas Theological Seminary. When asked to explain his philosophy of coaching, he said that the job of a coach is to make men do what they don't want to do so that they can achieve what they've always wanted. That's what Jesus does for you and me. He continually puts us in places we don't want to go and He makes us face things we don't want to face in order to achieve in us what we always wanted but didn't know how to find. This is a blessing no one wants but everyone needs if our faith is to grow and mature. If desperate circumstances bring us to Jesus, then those circumstances are a gift from God.

CHAPTER 10

His Faithfulness to Finish His Work in You

T he life of a Christian is a series of miracles." So said Charles Haddon Spurgeon, the great British preacher of the nineteenth century. If he is correct, why don't we ever talk about those miracles? In attempting to answer that question, I asked several friends to tell me about the miracles they had personally experienced. All of the stories were inspiring, and some were very instructive. Here is one man's story:

> If I had asked a close friend 16 years ago to write down a description of me and then do the same today, here is the conclusion you would have come to once you read them: These are two distinctly different people with very little in common. What happened? Nothing short of a miracle! I won't go into all the details, but 16 years ago I was at the end of my emotional and spiritual rope. One day I got down on my knees and told God to either change me or take me home because I didn't want to live another minute if my life was going to be the same as it had been. That's when I started to hear the faint sounds of hammering and sawing inside.

To jump to the end of the story, over the last 16 years God has created a whole new person inside this one. That's not visible to most folks. And it wasn't in the twinkling of an eye. But it is a miracle! It is spectacular! And it isn't over yet! What God has done in my life is more miraculous than if He had grown a new arm or leg to replace an amputated one—because He has grown a whole new person. He still does miracles! They are spectacular! They are in His time! To God be the glory!

As I read this man's story, the thought occurred to me that there are miracles all around us if only we had eyes to see them. *Our problem is that we look for outward, spectacular results when God's work, like the tiny mustard seed, begins in a hidden place inside the human heart.* As wonderful as reports of physical healing are—and I thank God that He still heals in answer to prayer today—the greater miracle is the transformation of a sinner into a saint by the grace of God.

I love one particular sentence in this man's testimony: "That's when I started to hear the faint sounds of hammering and sawing inside." If you have been a believer for any length of time, you already know about that hammering and sawing inside your own life. Theologians have a big word for it. They call it *sanctification*. It's the work God does inside the heart of a believer in order to make him more and more like Christ.

Here are five fast facts you need to know about sanctification:

- It is the work of God.

- It is a lifelong process.

- It is never complete in this life.

- God won't stop until the job is done.

- God uses everything that happens to us—the good and the bad—to make us like Jesus.

The Lord's Involvement in Our Growth

As a place to hang our thoughts, let's take a quick look at four Bible passages that speak of God's determination to finish His work in us.

1. *He Starts the Work in Us*

"Being confident of this, that he who began a good work in you will carry it on to completion until the day of Christ Jesus" (Philippians 1:6).

We need to note three things about this much-quoted verse. *First, God takes the initiative in starting His work in you.* He is the one who "begins a good work" in us. Salvation always begins with God. He makes the first move, and if He didn't make the first move, we would make no move at all.

Perhaps you've heard of the country preacher who was being examined for ordination to the ministry. When asked how he had become a Christian, the preacher replied, "I did my part, and God did His." That sounded questionable, so the learned brethren on the council asked the preacher to explain "his part in salvation." "My part was to run from God as fast as I could," the preacher answered. "God's part was to run after me and catch me and bring me into His family." That's a perfectly biblical answer because all of us were born running from God—if God hadn't taken the initiative to find us, we would still be running away from Him.

Second, God takes personal responsibility for completing His work in you. I find this a most comforting thought. God has a "good work" that He intends to accomplish in your life and in mine. As Romans 8:29 says, God intends that all His children be conformed to the image of Jesus Christ, and He will not rest until that "good work" is finally finished.

Perhaps you've seen those buttons that read PBPGIF WMY. Those cryptic letters stand for: "Please be patient. God isn't finished with me yet." Thank God, it's true. I may not look like much—but God isn't finished with me yet. And when you look in the mirror—and even deeper into your soul—you may not like what you see, but no matter. God isn't finished with you yet. There is good news and bad news in this truth. The good news is that because God isn't finished yet, we have great hope for the future. The bad news is that because God isn't finished yet, He won't let us stay as we are today. He's going to keep chipping away at us until we are conformed to the image of Jesus Christ. For all of us, it's a lifelong journey—and some of us have an enormous distance to travel. But that doesn't matter. If you find yourself in the muck and mire of personal defeat, be encouraged. Child of God, He's not finished with you yet. Rise and walk, my Christian friend. God is not finished with you yet. If you've been sent to the bench for a personal foul, learn the lesson God has for you and then get back in the game.

Third, God guarantees the outcome of His work in you. Not only does God start the process and continue the process, He also guarantees its ultimate outcome. He will "carry it on to completion until the day of Christ Jesus" (Philippians 1:6). This means that God won't be turned aside by difficulties of any kind. He is so determined to make you like Jesus that even your own backsliding won't hinder the accomplishment of His purpose. Someday you and I will stand before Jesus Christ as redeemed children of God— holy, blameless, and complete in every way. We're a far sight from that today, but a better day is coming for us. What is incomplete will be made complete. What is unfinished will be finished. What is lacking will be made full. What is partial will be made whole. What is less than enough will be far more than adequate. What is broken will be fixed. What is hurt will be healed. What is weak will be made strong. What is temporary will be made permanent.

God has promised to do it and He cannot lie. God has begun a good work in your life. Do you feel incomplete and unfinished? Fear not, child of God. He will complete His work in you.

2. He Keeps Us from Falling

"To him who is able to keep you from falling and to present you before his glorious presence without fault and with great joy" (Jude 24).

In this verse there are three elements we need to observe:

First, there is the *power* of God: "To him who is able to keep you from falling."

Second, there is the *purpose* of God: "To present you before his glorious presence."

Third, there is the *promise* of God: "Without fault and with great joy."

God has ordained that those whom He calls to salvation will be so preserved that though they stumble along the way, they will not utterly fall away. He guards His children by His Spirit and with the holy angels to ensure that none are lost during their earthly pilgrimage. As many as God calls, that many will He one day receive in heaven. I love the way J. Vernon McGee used to put it. Dr. McGee pictured the Lord in heaven counting His sheep as they come into the fold: "...94...95...96...97...98...99...McGee? Where's McGee? I can't find him!" No, McGee would say, it's not like that. All of God's sheep will make it. Not one will be lost in the process.

Bible teacher Jack Wyrtzen put it this way: "I'm as sure of heaven as if I'd already been there 10,000 years." How can a Christian say that? Because our assurance doesn't rest on you or me. *It rests on the word of the eternal God.* If God has said He's going to do it, He will do it. You can take it to the bank. What God says He will do, He will do. Jude 24 says that God's purpose is to present us before the Lord without a single blemish. The Greek word for "without fault" has in mind the temple sacrifices. It describes a lamb that is free from all defects. No cuts, no broken bones, no spots, no diseases of any kind. God said, "Bring Me a lamb without spot, or don't bring one at all." He rejects defective sacrifices as unworthy of His holiness.

But if that is true, then how will any of us stand before the Lord? We all have spots, blemishes, secret faults, hidden sins, wrong attitudes, bad habits, and sin that hangs around our necks like a heavy weight. We're all struggling to make it from one day to the next, and many of us live with a guilty conscience and a keen sense of our own failure. And that's when we need to remember the truth in Jude 24: God intends to present us before His own throne faultless, spotless, free from everything in this life that drags us down. In that great day the angels will hush their singing as, one by one, the saints of God are introduced to our heavenly Father. I picture the Lord Jesus saying, "Father, this is Stan Utigard. He has just come from a hard struggle on the earth. By virtue of My blood, I present him to You perfect, spotless, and without any blemish." And the Father will say, "Well done, good and faithful servant. Enter into the joy of the Lord."

So it will be for all those who know Jesus Christ. But what about our sins? They are covered by the blood of Jesus and were judged at the cross. All the failures of this life will be left far behind. All the undone work of a lifetime will be but a dim memory—if we remember it at all. In that great day, we will be completely delivered from sin and all its devastation.

Don't skip over the little phrase "with great joy." In the Greek text it means something like "with unbridled exultation." When the saints go marching in, it will be like one of those noisy parades in New Orleans (only without the bad stuff). We will enter heaven not with downcast eyes and somber faces, but singing and laughing and with shouts of eternal joy. "Hallelujah, by the grace of God, we made it!" When sin torments you this week, let this thought encourage you. *Better days are coming.* Days of victory. Days of rejoicing are not far away. Your present failure won't last forever. One day the battle will be over and you will stand in God's presence whole and complete. You will enter heaven with a song on your lips; God has willed it so.

3. *He Equips Us to Do His Will*

"May the God of peace, who through the blood of the eternal covenant brought back from the dead our Lord Jesus, that great Shepherd of the sheep, equip you with everything good for doing his will, and may he work in us what is pleasing to him, through Jesus Christ, to whom be glory for ever and ever. Amen" (Hebrews 13:20-21).

The word "equip" means "to restore to proper working condition." The word was used to speak of getting an army ready for battle or sewing up a hole in a fishing net or setting an arm that was broken. You equip something when you prepare it to be used for its proper purpose.

God is willing to equip us to do everything He wants us to do. Let me flip that statement over: *God will never call us to do something without also equipping us to do it.* Never. He simply will not do it. I know many people who today face difficult situations. Perhaps you do, too. You may be out of money. You may be out of a job. You may be facing surgery

very soon, or a debilitating illness. You may have hard decisions you need to make this week and you have no idea
what to do. Take this word of cheer: Whatever you have to
do this week, God will equip you to do it. No matter how
hard the road ahead, God has already started mending your
nets and arming you for battle. You don't even have to ask
Him; He just does it because that's the kind of God He is. He
never, never, never calls you to any hard task without giving
you what you need to get the job done.

And notice how He does it. He works in us from the
inside out: "May he work *in us* what is pleasing to him"
(emphasis added). If we need courage, He works that in us.
If we need compassion, He gives it to us. If we need
integrity, He builds it in. If we need wisdom, He imparts the
wisdom. If we need common sense, He finds a way to give
it to us. So many of us look at a difficult situation and pray,
"Lord, change my situation." That's not usually God's will.
Much more often the difficult situation has come as a means
of making us grow spiritually. *God often brings difficulty into
our lives to deepen our total dependence on Him.* When that
happens, we ought to pray, "Lord, change me so that I can
face this situation." That's a prayer God is pleased to answer.

4. *He Promises to Complete His Work in Us*

*"May God himself, the God of peace, sanctify you through
and through. May your whole spirit, soul and body be kept
blameless at the coming of our Lord Jesus Christ. The one who
calls you is faithful and he will do it"* (1 Thessalonians 5:23-
24).

How do we know that God will finish what He starts in
us? In legal terms, God is the "guarantor," the one who
stands behind the promise. Just as any contract is only worth
the integrity of the name on the paper, even so our hope of
sanctification is only as good as the person who stands
behind it. In this case, we know our sanctification is certain

because Paul uses an emphatic Greek construction in the text to drive his point home:

God

God Himself

God Himself, the God of peace

Here is yet another important truth: *Only God can make you better.* Think about that for a moment. Exercise may improve your body, therapy may help your soul, friends may lift your spirit, good fortune may improve your circumstances, but only God can make you better.

God is the author and source of all spiritual progress. It is impossible to overstate the importance of this fundamental truth. Our problem is that we try to make ourselves better in our own power. So we struggle mightily to overcome a drinking problem, a vicious temper, an unforgiving spirit, a critical tongue, or some other evil habit. In our battle against sin we crawl into a corner and try to get better on our own. After a while we stand up and say, "See how nice I look, Lord? And I did it all by myself." And from the heavens comes this reply: "Without Me you can do nothing." In contrast to all our feeble efforts at moral betterment and self-improvement, this text simply says, "God himself, the God of peace." It starts with God, and if it doesn't start there, you haven't really started at all.

God's Thoroughness in Our Growth

The little phrase "through and through" is translated from an unusual two-part Greek word. One part means "whole," and the other means "complete" or "at the end." It refers to being wholly sanctified so that in the end you will be made complete. God has ordained that His children—*all* of them without exception—will be made complete in the end. We're not that way now. Most of us feel fragmented and torn in many directions. We're incomplete and under construction in this life. But God intends that when we finally get to heaven, the hammers and saws will be put away and we will stand before the Lord with every part perfectly in place and every aspect of our life made perfect.

Sanctification is a process leading to a product. Years ago there was a little chorus that went this way: "Little by little, day by day, little by little, in every way, Jesus is changing me." That's the way it is for all of us. We grow little by little and we make progress day by day. It's not very fast, but the Lord is never in a hurry. He takes His time because He is the Master Craftsman.

Sometimes careless workmen will say, "That's close enough." That's a way of saying, "Don't worry about the details. The joints don't have to fit, the margins can be crooked, we don't need to worry about the budget. We don't have to be perfect; we don't even have to be close." Mark it down plainly: God is not a careless workman. Everything He does is perfect. But most of us don't feel very "perfect" right now. We look inside and see lots of good and bad mixed together and many loose connections and a lot of parts that don't seem to work or fit right. But we won't be that way forever. God has promised that in the end, we will be sanctified through and through.

We're not finished yet, but we will be.

We're not completely clean today, but we will be.

We're not wholly wise today, but we will be.

We're not totally redeemed right now, but we will be.

We're not always useful to God, but we will be.

We can thus be fully confident that when Jesus returns, two great things will happen for every believer: Our character will be revealed, and our perfection will be complete.

Along the way, however, you may feel as if you're making slow progress. Do you ever get discouraged about your own life? I do. Do you ever stand in front of a mirror and say, "What's wrong with you? Why aren't you getting better?" Sometimes it seems as if the Christian life is three steps forward and two steps back. Spiritual growth can be discouraging at times. It's like climbing Mount Everest: the closer you get to the top, the farther away it seems. But God has reasons for all this. He wants us to depend on Him for everything. He designed life so that it works only when we allow Him to be in total charge of everything. When we try to run the show—which we often do—things begin to fall apart.

God's Intention in Our Growth

While commenting on 1 Thessalonians 5:23-24 some 350 years ago, John Calvin used a picturesque expression. He said that God intends "the entire renovation of the man." I never understood *renovation* until I moved to Oak Park in 1989. Now I know what it means because everything in this village is under constant renovation! Around here, a "new" house is only 70 years old and an average house is 80 years old. An "old" house is at least 100 years old. That's why anyone who can renovate old buildings does big business in Oak Park. People who live in older homes know what I mean. You never really get the job finished. First you work on the roof, then you start on the living room, then the kitchen, then the bedrooms one by one. Probably you'll have trouble with the plumbing and the electrical system (more than once!). Eventually you'll have to replace the porch, repaint the trim, and install a new heater and maybe even an air conditioner. If you don't know what I'm talking about, take my word for it: The job is never done. You can work on a house for 15–20 years and still not be completely finished. There's always something else to do.

If you think houses are hard, imagine renovating a human life. That's a job so tough only God would attempt it. No matter how long you've been under renovation—25 years, 30 years, 40 years, or 50-plus years, the job won't be done until you are in heaven. I've sometimes wondered if God eventually says to some people, "I've done all I can do down there. Come on up here and I'll finish the job where the working conditions are much better." (In truth, that's what He eventually says to all of us.)

God's Faithfulness to Our Growth

There's a very important phrase tucked away in 1 Thessalonians 5:24: "The one who calls you is faithful." This is the foundation for the doctrine of eternal security. We like to say that those who are saved are saved forever. But how do we know this is true? We know it because God is faithful to keep His promises. Our entire hope—both in this life and in the life to come—rests on the faithfulness of God. His faithfulness bears the entire weight of our puny efforts. You are a work-in-process, and so am I. We're all "under construction." And remember that construction is long, loud, noisy, and even messy. That's why most of us can hear the sound of hammering and sawing on the inside. God never stops His work because there is always room for us to grow more Christlike.

- If you concentrate on your weakness, you will lose your confidence.

- If you concentrate on God's faithfulness, you will grow in confidence.

In my mind's eye, I picture God as a sculptor working with a rough piece of marble. He's working on a big chunk named Ray Pritchard. It's a hard job because the chunk is badly marred, misshapen, discolored, and cracked in odd places. It's about the worst piece of marble a sculptor could ever find. But God is undeterred and He's working patiently at His job, chipping away the bad parts, chiseling an image into the hard stone, stopping occasionally to polish here and there. One day He finally finishes one portion of the statue. The next morning when He returns to the studio, that portion is messed up. "I thought I finished that yesterday," He says. "Who's been messing with My statue?" With a guilty grin, I raise my hand. It turns out that I'm the culprit. I'm my own worst enemy. What I thought would improve things has only messed them up. But God is faithful. He patiently picks up His chisel and goes back to work. He won't quit halfway through a project.

When I asked Barb Duncan to share her experience of God's faithfulness, she wrote about the many times she and her husband, Wally, have been delivered from various health problems, including colon cancer, being knifed by muggers, a heart attack, and six major surgeries. She also mentioned two job losses and considerable financial uncertainty. Then she added these words:

> The strange thing is that when you asked for stories of God's faithfulness, all I can describe is the many small ways that God has gotten us through each day. The rainbow, a check that came unexpectedly through the mail, a timely or convicting word that applied, a successful surgery. God's faithfulness has just flooded my life, made up of the thousands of tiny raindrops of His precious presence through every day and in every situation.

But even that was not the bottom line:

I learned that God's faithfulness to His promises
was not dependent on how I was feeling; that He
wasn't going to vacillate with my every doubt or
discouragement. I learned that in our most painful
times, we begin to pray with a passion and listen
far more intently to the voice of a living, interac-
tive God. The relationship that has developed with
Him has been far more the answer than all the
gifts He has bestowed.

Barb's last sentence catches the spirit of 1 Thessalonians
5:23-24. God is so faithful that He goes far beyond answering
our prayers and supplying our needs. He wants us to understand that *He Himself* is the answer we need.

God's Promise to Complete Our Growth

Note the last four words of 1 Thessalonians 5:24: "He
will do it." They are simple and direct. No qualification, no
hesitation, no doubt of any kind. Just four simple words:
"He will do it." Not "He *may* do it" or "He *might* do it" or
"He *could* do it" or "He will do it *if He feels like it.*" Not even
"He will do it *if we do our part.*" Just a simple declarative
statement that God *will* do it. Unqualified by even the
slightest reference to anything on our part. When it's all said
and done, what matters is not my strong hold on God, but
His strong hold on me.

Sometimes when I ask someone, "How are you?" the
reply comes, "I'm doing all right." That's a conversational
nicety, but it's not accurate. If the truth be told, much of the
time, we're not all right. Some of us feel all right and most
of us feel partly right and partly wrong. But none of us are
completely all right in every area of life. For the moment
we're not all right, but by God's grace, we're moving in that
direction and, in the end, all God's children are going to be

all right when we stand in His presence. In that day, we will be whole and complete—pure and perfected. No more hammering, no more sawing, no more polishing. Why? Because God finishes what He starts.

We may chafe, doubt, and despair of any progress at all. We may be angry and give up. But God does not change. He is faithful, and He will complete His work in us. What is left for us? *Simply to place ourselves in God's hands.* To cooperate with the Master Designer as He shapes us into the image of Jesus. To say, "Lord, here I am. Make me what You want me to be."

Take heart. God is at work in your life. And He will not stop until the job is done.

CHAPTER 11

His Faithfulness to Every Generation

D o you know where you were 33 years ago today? On almost any other day of the year I would not be able to answer that question, but on this particular day I know the answer. Thirty-three years ago today I was attending a youth retreat at Tishimingo State Park in northeastern Mississippi. As I am writing these words, today is Thursday, but 33 years ago, it was Saturday. I remember bits and pieces of that weekend. Even though I was still a high school student, I was asked to speak on Friday night. I think the theme was "Mission: Impossible," but I don't have a clue what I said. Thankfully it wasn't taped, and I didn't save any notes. On Saturday a group of college students from the University of Alabama came to speak to us. I recall that they were part of a group I had never heard of before—Campus Crusade for Christ. When they shared how they had come to know Christ personally, I was blown away. Even though I had been raised in an evangelical church, I had never heard anyone talk about *knowing* Christ as they did. I can't remember anything in particular that they said, with one exception. One of the students finished his talk by saying, "It's time to get on the stick, and Christ is the stick." I'm still pondering that one a third of a century later.

The next day, we returned to the small town in Alabama where I grew up. Something happened to me that weekend that changed my life so that it has remained changed ever since. Looking back, I think it was the difference between what I saw in my own life (not much) versus what I saw in the lives of those enthusiastic college students. I had religion; they knew the Lord. And even if they weren't the most eloquent ambassadors in the world, their genuine faith came shining through, and in the process it revealed the emptiness of my own life. Sometime that weekend the scales fell from my eyes and I realized that I was not saved, even though I was religious and baptized and a church member and had done everything the youth group wanted me to do. I did not know the Lord. If you ask, "How did you feel?" I would have to say I felt relieved—the way you feel when you go to the doctor and he finally tells you what's wrong. I went home when the retreat was over, still thinking. I must have gotten up and gone to church the next morning, but I don't remember it.

That Sunday afternoon I realized that I needed to do some business with Jesus. I didn't know what to do. But one moment remains etched in my memory. Late that Sunday afternoon, around 5:15 P.M., I walked out the front door of my house and sat on the concrete steps by myself. After thinking things over, I bowed my head and said, "Jesus, if You are real, come into my life. Amen." Then I got up and walked away. If anyone had seen me, they wouldn't have suspected what was happening. And I wasn't sure myself. I didn't hear the angels sing; I didn't hear the voice of God. But I do remember a tingling feeling on the inside, a sense of expectation when you've just done something important and you want to know what is going to happen next.

Not knowing what else to do, I walked inside my house, picked up my Bible, and flipped it open to 1 John. I'm not sure why I did that, but I found out later that 1 John is a great book for new Christians to read because it is written to help people find assurance of eternal life.

And that's how my Christian life began 33 years ago. A third of a century has come and gone, and the decision I made as a teenager still marks my life today. I am what I am because of what happened when I prayed a very simple prayer on the concrete steps outside my house one Sunday afternoon a long time ago.

Pondering God's Past Faithfulness

A Midnight Encounter with God

A year passed and I graduated from high school. In my heart I had a great love for journalism. Back then, Walter Cronkite was my hero, and I dreamed of someday being on radio or television. I was bound for the University of Missouri, where I planned to study journalism. But as Proverbs 16:9 says, "In his heart a man plans his course, but the LORD determines his steps." This verse doesn't say that God *directs* our steps (although that is true—see Proverbs 3:6 KJV), but rather, that God *determines* our steps. This is a very strong word that speaks of God's control of every detail in the universe. Perhaps you've heard it said that "man proposes, but God disposes." *You can make all your plans—in fact, you can have your life mapped out step by step—but in the end, God determines every step you take.* After we have made our plans, we don't know if they will succeed, if they should succeed, or even if we would be happier if they succeeded or failed. Our plans change because we change, our circumstances change, and the people around us change. How comforting it is to know that in the midst of our confusion, God determines the steps we take.

It was almost exactly a year after my Sunday afternoon prayer that the Lord spoke to me again. This time it was late at night, after my family had gone to bed. I remember that in the month after my high school graduation, I used to stay up late, pacing my room, wondering what I should do with my life. There were so many choices, so many roads leading to exciting destinations. Which one should I take? Though I wasn't aware of it at the time, God was calling me into the ministry. Late one night, after pacing the floor for a while, I went to sleep. *Sometime during the night I awoke and knew that God was calling me.* I can't tell how I knew, but I knew with the kind of certainty that comes when the God of the universe knocks on the door of your heart. It occurs to me as I write these words that some people will simply not understand what I am saying. I did not have an "experience" that night in an emotional sense. I didn't hear or see anything. But I remember being certain that God was calling me and that I had to respond. So I said, "Lord, if You want me, I'll be a preacher." Then I went back to sleep—just as short and simple as that. But when I awoke the next morning, I knew that "something" had happened and my life had been redirected.

Married in Six Weeks

Four years later, in the same month of the year, Marlene and I sat on the big king-size bed in my parents' bedroom and told them we wanted to get married. In six weeks. In Phoenix, Arizona. Mom gasped a bit; Dad just smiled. I don't think he was surprised at all. I was young and in love, a college graduate, about to go to seminary in the fall, and I didn't have any time to waste. I had found a beautiful woman who loved me and was willing to become my wife, so why wait? After talking it over, they agreed we should get married in six weeks.

So now the clock of life runs forward 15 years. In the interim we were married, my father died shortly thereafter, I started and finished seminary, we moved to California (where our first two sons were born), and we moved to

Texas (where our third son was born). After 15 years, in the same month of the year, I was about to go for a candidating visit to a church in Oak Park, Illinois. How that came about is a story so convoluted that I don't have time to tell it. I can summarize it by simply saying that if God had not wanted it to happen, I could never have orchestrated it myself. The candidating seemed to go fairly well. Now we wondered what the church would do, and if we were about to be uprooted and moved to Chicago. I remember telling the pulpit committee that I wouldn't come without at least a 90 percent vote from the congregation. That seemed a likely way out (if we needed one), because some people feel the apostle Paul couldn't have gotten a 90 percent vote from a pulpit committee. The vote was over 90 percent, so we packed our bags and moved from Garland, Texas, to Oak Park, Illinois. It would be very fair to say that I made the move with a sense of trepidation. How would I, a Southern boy, fit in up North, in Chicago of all places, in a part of the country that was very different than where I came from? Looking back, I think I wouldn't have come at all except that I sensed God was leading us to this place.

Looking Back, Looking Ahead

Now 13 years have passed. If you were to ask me what has happened during those 13 years, the answer is nothing and everything. Back then I was 36 years old and had no gray hair; today I am almost 50 and am graying slowly and gracefully (I hope). Back then my boys were 4, 7, and 9. Today I have a high school senior, a college sophomore, and a college graduate. Back then I had no inkling that Marlene would be the full-time administrator of a Christian school, one that didn't even exist at the time. I had no clue of what was to come when I loaded my Honda and made the long trip north.

Such is my life so far. As of this writing...

Thirty-three years ago tomorrow I became a Christian.

Thirty-two years ago this month I was called to the ministry.

Twenty-eight years ago this month Marlene and I decided to get married in six weeks.

Thirteen years ago this month I was a pastoral candidate at the church I now pastor.

Who knows what tomorrow holds? I certainly don't. I agree with my friend who recently told me, "God didn't give me a videotape of the future." I'm glad I didn't know 33 years ago all that would happen to me. Too much of it would have made no sense in advance, and some of it would have frightened me. Life is always better lived one day at a time. That way we can leave the future in God's hands, where it belongs.

Looking back, I can clearly see the hand of God every step of the way. Some things still don't make sense to me, like my father's death a few weeks after we were married. But I see clearly that the Lord was leading us to move our wedding date forward so Dad could be my best man. The rest of it—why he got sick and why he died when he did— remains a mystery to me. But I don't have to know the answers in order to be happy or content. *When I think about the mysteries of life, I find myself satisfied to worship a God whose ways are so awesome that He feels no need to explain Himself fully to me.* A God I could fully understand would not be worth worshiping.

Fifty and Counting!

By the time you read this, I will have passed my fiftieth birthday. And like many men at this point in life, I have been taking stock, looking back, looking around, and trying to look ahead. I know that I want my remaining years, however many or few they may be, to count for the Lord. I hope to be around long enough to see my boys find Christian wives and settle down on their own. And I have asked the Lord to let me live long enough to see my grandchildren playing at my feet. If God wills it so, then perhaps Marlene and I will grow old together. Maybe we'll celebrate our fiftieth wedding anniversary 22 years from now. I hope so, but I know there are no guarantees about any of this. The future is hidden in the heart and mind of God.

But this much I know: *God has been faithful to me.* His faithfulness started long before 33 years ago, and it will continue long after my earthly life is over. When I am in heaven, He will still be faithful to my children, to my yet-to-be-born grandchildren, and to the great-grandchildren I believe God will send many years from now. Whether I live to see them or not, my great-grandchildren (and the generations after them) will experience the same faithfulness of God that I have known. This is a promise of God that spans the generations.

Praising God's Continuing Faithfulness

To learn more about God's continuing faithfulness, let's take a look at Psalm 100. Many years ago this psalm was sung to a tune called "The Old Hundredth." Today we know the tune better as "The Doxology." You can find a musical version of Psalm 100 in most hymnals, usually under the title "All Creatures That on Earth Do Dwell." The Hebrew text calls it "A psalm for giving thanks." Even though there are many thanksgiving psalms, this is the only one specifically titled that way. It is sometimes called the "Jubilate," which means "O be joyful." In Old Testament times, the Jews used this psalm as part of the temple worship. The same is true in the Christian era, especially as part of liturgical worship.

Thus these simple words have blessed the hearts of God's people for nearly 3000 years.

The Reasons for Praising God's Faithfulness

I would like to focus our attention on the last verse in Psalm 100, which gives us three reasons to praise God: "The LORD is good and his love endures forever; his faithfulness continues through all generations" (verse 5).

Reason #1: The Lord Is Good

"For the LORD is good." This speaks of God's character—that God is good, and all He does is good. I realize I do not know your personal circumstances. You may be in a difficult place and wonder if things will ever get better. While I don't know the particulars of your situation, I do know this: *God has been good to you.* In Nigeria (and in other parts of Africa), pastors teach this truth to their congregation using a simple antiphonal chant. The pastor will proclaim, "God is good," and the congregation responds with one voice, "All the time." Then the pastor says, "All the time," and the congregation replies, "God is good." What a powerful and important affirmation that is! Not just that God is good—this much we already know—but to declare out loud and in one voice that "all the time" and in every circumstance our God is good.

Everything we see around us confirms this truth. Sometimes God's goodness is seen quickly, other times it is seen slowly as we ponder the mysterious ways of God's divine providence. Eventually we come to realize that nothing leaves God's hand that does not touch His goodness in one way or the other. I'm sure we could all make a list of reasons to give thanks to God: for family, friends, good health, good grades, a good job, a good report from the doctor, and so on. However, Psalm 100 asks us to praise God simply because He is good. This is the highest form of praise—when we praise God not for what He does, but for who He is.

God did not create us because of any lack within Himself. He created us because He desired to share His own image with us. He did not have to do that, but He did because that's the kind of God He is. "He made us, and we are His," says the psalmist. *The very fact of your existence proves God's goodness.* He cared enough to create you, and then He cared enough to send His Son to die for you. Surely God is good all the time. And all the time, God is good.

Reason #2: His Love Endures

"His love endures forever." Some translations use the word "mercy" instead of "love." If God's goodness speaks of His *character,* God's mercy speaks of His *nature.* Mercy is God's goodness in relation to sin~~ ~~He forgives sins both now and in the future. P   ercy endures forever, it has no beginni~~   ~~ time began, He was the eternal Fat~~   ~~od is eternal, His mercy exte~~   ~~mind can conceive…a~~   ~~is finally done—if~~   ~~mercy will st~~   ~~ed, an~~   ~~f

d~~   ~~
on ~~   ~~
can d~~   ~~
you can ~~   ~~
and His lov

We see G~~   ~~
While walking ~~   ~~with
this saying on it: ~~   ~~ou love
me?' 'This much,' H~~   ~~ed out His

arms and died." Fix your eyes upon the bloody cross of Calvary. Gaze upon the dying form of the Son of God. There you will find grace unmeasured, mercy undeserved, and love beyond degree.

A few days ago I received an e-mail message from someone who shared a bit of her personal story and her struggle to live for the Lord. Here is a portion of her last paragraph:

> Your messages on God being faithful to the fallen and the tempted shook me in my very seat (sometimes I feel as if you have a spotlight on me and wish you would shut it off because everyone knows you are speaking to me). But your message on God finishing what He starts really helped in a way you will never realize. To know that God will do something with me is joy enough. I often feel like I am just trudging through my days, waiting for something miraculous to happen, just hoping that I won't fall into some other great sin. "If I could just make it to Sunday, then I will be okay" has been my plea for many years. But now knowing that God actually wants to do something with me has rekindled a little more faith for my future. God's truly amazing grace is so simple. When understood it is all based on His love, and no matter what I do (or don't do), no matter who I struggle with becoming, and no matter what I do to mess everything up, He still has a plan for me. What an awesome God I serve!

That's the difference God's love can make. His mercy endures forever.

Reason #3: His Faithfulness Continues

"His faithfulness continues through all generations." This final phrase speaks of God's promise to us. We can face the future with confidence because His faithfulness continues from one generation to another. Some translations say "his truth endures." That's entirely correct because God's truth and His faithfulness both spring from His unchanging nature. Consider what it means to say that His truth endures:

> *He is true in Himself.* There is no deceit and no falsehood in God. No error can be found in His nature.

> *He is true in His dealing with His creation.*

> *He is true in His dealing with humanity.*

> *He is true in all His promises.*

Where can you find a promise God has not kept? What has He spoken that has not come to pass?

No changes, however great, can produce any changes in God. All things are moving according to His divine plan. There are no mistakes with the Lord. You may think it otherwise, but it is not true. You may say, "All things are against me," but it is not so. All things are for you, but you do not yet see it. God is ordering all for the best.

Consider the last words: "through all generations." This literally means "from generation to generation." Exodus 20:6 tells us that God shows His love to "a thousand generations" of those who love Him. If we assume that a generation equals 40 years, then God's love lasts at least 40,000 years. And because this promise was given to Moses at Mount Sinai approximately 3500 years ago, we may safely conclude that God's faithful love will continue at least another 36,500 years. That is to say, with 3500 years having gone by, we are not even 10 percent of the way through the length of God's love. "But surely that is not literal," you say. Indeed, it is not. But it is not purely figurative either. This passage is showing us that God's love and faithfulness go far beyond human comprehension.

The Assurance Inherent in God's Faithfulness

Suppose we line up a grandfather, a father, a son, a grandson, and a great-grandson next to each other. Psalm 100 tells us that what God is to the grandfather, He will be to the father. What He is to the father, He will be to the son. What He is to the son, He will be to the grandson. What He is to the grandson, He will be to the great-grandson. And so it goes across the centuries. Generations come and go, one after the other. Only God remains forever.

This is our hope at the edge of death. This is why we rejoice as we bury our dead. As I think back across my quarter century as a pastor, I remember the solemn privilege that has been mine to lay to rest some of the greatest saints of God I have ever known. It has been well said that nothing of God dies when a man or woman of God dies. *We need not fear death because a Christian is immortal until his work on earth is done.* You cannot die and you will not die until God's appointed time for you finally arrives. Until then, you are immortal.

Shortly before Eugenie Longinow died, Marlene and I visited her at West Suburban Hospital in Oak Park. She and her husband had come to the United States from Europe shortly after World Word II. They learned to speak English by listening to a Christian radio station in Chicago. When we saw her, it was clear that she didn't have long to live. She couldn't talk very well, but she knew who we were, and when we began to recite Psalm 23, she tried to say it along with us. I called John Sergey, one of our elders, and told him that I thought she was going to die that night. I'll never forget his prayer at the end of our conversation: "We thank Thee, Lord, for the death of the saints of God. Some go before and some after, but one by one your children pass from this life directly into Your presence." I don't think I had ever heard anyone give thanks for the death of God's saints, but it is entirely biblical, and John's prayer lifted my heart.

I do not know how much time we have left until we reach the end of our earthly road. But this I know: That road is paved with God's love and faithfulness. And we need not be afraid.

I am so glad that God's faithfulness transcends the generations. I am 50 years old, heading for...what? 55? 60? 75? Maybe 80 or even 90 years old if God blesses me with long life. But I won't live forever. As the years roll by, I find myself realizing how much of my life is wrapped up in my three boys. Today they are in their teens and early 20s, tomorrow they will be fully grown with families of their own, and the day after that they will be grandfathers.

Will God still take care of them? What about their children? And their grandchildren? Will God still be there for them? *The answer is yes because God's faithfulness doesn't depend on me but on His character, which spans the generations.* That means I don't have to stay alive to ensure that my boys will be okay. God will see to that. After I am gone from this earth, and even if all my prayers have not been answered, I can trust God to take care of my boys. What a comfort this is. I can do my best to help my boys while I'm here, and after I'm gone God's faithfulness will continue for them and for their grandchildren, and even for their great-grandchildren.

While I was pondering all of that, a poignant thought came to my mind. If I were dying and had just 30 seconds to pass along my highest values to my three sons, what would I say? Very quickly, four things came to my mind:

1. Take care of your mother.

2. Love each other.

3. Marry Christian girls.

4. Serve Jesus Christ forever.

That summarizes all I really care about. If my boys will do these things, I'll die feeling like my life has been well spent. The wonderful thing is this: God has promised to be faithful to every generation. If my values are weak, that promise becomes punishment; but if my values reflect God's values, then that promise becomes my best hope for the future.

Because God is faithful, we can trust Him with the generations yet to come. Here is great hope for parents who worry about their children: The God who cares for us will take care of our children—and their children's children—too.

Recognizing God's Ongoing Faithfulness

While I was working on this book, my friend Chris Jahns wrote to tell me about God's faithfulness to his family across the generations. Several years ago there was a Jahns family reunion at Deer Valley Ranch in Colorado involving 50 people on his father's side of the family. Chris's father and his two siblings had a believing mother who, during her early twenties, had been far from the Lord and had married a nonbeliever. She came back to the Lord soon after, and committed to the Lord and to her husband that she was going to faithfully raise her children for the Lord. She was a quiet, loving, faithful, praying woman. She died when Chris was a child. But through her faithfulness and prayers for her extended family in a less-than-ideal marital situation (believer and unbeliever), God was very faithful to her. As a result, her three children all grew up as strong believers (elders, teachers in their local churches), all 11 grandchildren (many of whom she never knew) are believers and serving God, and all of her 20-plus great grandchildren (none of whom she ever knew) are followers of Christ. Often during child dedications I will pray that "the stream of Christian truth that starts today will last to the third and fourth generations," and I add that "we will not all live to see the answer to this prayer." Chris wrote that his grandmother was a perfect example of how God works across the generations. She prayed, yet saw only the beginning of the answers.

Chris went on to say that the heritage passed down to him was not the result of good parenting or good luck. "This was the blessing of God because of prayer and faithfulness through several generations, and with that came great responsibility for the coming generations." In the Old Testament, the people of God often built memorial altars to help them remember significant moments in their spiritual journey. Wanting to make sure his children shared in that spiritual heritage and to someday pass it on to their children, Chris planned a special event for their family reunion high in the Colorado mountains. The entire family took a trek to a remote area. There they talked about God's faithfulness to their family and how they must not take it for granted. Then the fathers of each generation came forward and the women and girls read Scripture. The men gathered in the middle and the women and girls and young sons gathered around them, laid their hands on them, and prayed that the men might be faithful to God, to their wives, their children, and that they might be given wisdom and strength from the Lord. Then the mothers stepped forward, the men read Scripture, and prayers were offered for the women. Then the children came forward and earnest prayers were offered for them—that they would be faithful to God and that God's truth would be passed on to the generations to come. Then the first generation talked to the younger members of the family about Chris's grandmother and great-grandfather, who loved God and were faithful to Him. At the end, everyone stood in a circle, joined hands, and sang "Great Is Thy Faithfulness." There were tears mixed with great joy as the family remembered God's faithfulness and vowed to pass it on to the generations yet to come.

I'll let Chris tell the end of the story in his own words:

> The final symbolic act we did was to grab stones (some of the big men grabbed big boulders and rolled them, others got smaller rocks) and made a monument to God. My cousins go back to the ranch every year, and they always go to that monument in the mountains to remind themselves of the commitments they made and their gratefulness to God for His faithfulness through the generations. The owners of the ranch will often take their guests to that location and tell the story (in fact, after the harsh winters, they go restack the rocks that may have moved or fallen so that the monument remains). It was one of the spiritual highlights of my life, and certainly in the lives of my kids and extended family.

Such a story is both a wonderful testimony and a powerful example that many other families should follow. *It is good for us to remember the blessings of the Lord and to celebrate His faithfulness that spans the generations.* And it is vital that we make sure our children and our children's children understand the heritage that has been passed down to them.

Resting in God's Enduring Faithfulness

As I grow older, I realize that I am less and less certain about some things and more and more certain about others. Here are three things I know for certain:

1. The Lord is good.

2. His mercy endures forever.

3. His faithfulness continues from generation to generation.

Is the Lord faithful? Can He be trusted in every circumstance? With all my heart, I believe the answer is yes. The Bible declares that God is faithful, and the saints of all the ages have proved that that is true. He can be trusted to keep His Word, and you can trust Him to do what He says He will do.

Giving In, Giving Up, or Giving Thanks

W. Tozer once remarked that "a thankful heart cannot be cynical." I paused when I read that because we live in such a cynical age. A cynic is a person who, having seen the bad side of human nature so often, finds it hard to take anything at face value. On one hand, such a person can be refreshingly realistic compared to the pie-in-the-sky dreamers who never question anything. The famous axiom of the newspaper reporter comes to mind: "If your mother says she loves you, check it out." Well, it's good to check things out and to have a healthy dose of skepticism when the voice on the phone offers you a "free" trip to Hawaii—that is, of course, if you'll just listen to a one-hour sales presentation.

A little cynicism can be good, but, like any virtue, it can quickly become a vice. And that brings me back to Tozer's brief remark. A heart of gratitude comes from realizing that God alone is the source of all our blessings. Everything else is derivative. I have what I have because God has willed me to have it. I live where I live because God has willed me to live here. I was born into a particular family because God willed it to be so. I was born in Tennessee, raised in Alabama, met my wife in Chattanooga, went to seminary in Dallas, and now live in Oak Park because God has willed it so. And even my problems (which aren't many) are apportioned to me by the hand of a loving God.

Life is a journey with many twists and turns, and as I get older, I find that I believe in the sovereignty of God more than ever before. That means there is no such thing as luck or fate or chance—not even in the tiniest things of life. And that God is in full control of the things that really matter—like life and death, health and sickness, and what the future holds for our loved ones. I heard about a little girl who, when asked what she had learned in Sunday school, said that she had learned that "God never says, 'Oops!'" That's comforting to know, because we live in an "Oops!" world where mistakes are made all the time, often by well-meaning people.

The cynic doubts that God knows or cares, and thus he gives in to doubt, anger, and sometimes to utter despair. But those who know their God know that He knows even when they don't know...and instead of giving in or giving up, they give thanks.

If you would like to contact the author, you can reach him in the following ways:

By letter: Ray Pritchard
             Calvary Memorial Church
             931 Lake Street
             Oak Park, IL 60301

By e-mail: PastorRay@calvarymemorial.com
Via the Internet: www.calvarymemorial.com